DOWNSIDE PROTECTION

PROCESS AND TENETS FOR SHORT SELLING IN ALL MARKET ENVIRONMENTS

Nitin K. Sacheti

Cover designed by Hiran Kuru

Edited by Julia Tofan

TABLE OF CONTENTS

ACKNOWLEDGEMENTS

Joe Grano for his guidance, Connie Kristan for her assistance with Papyrus Capital, my parents for their support, Michael Klett for encouraging me to launch the fund and all of our Year 1 investors for entrusting a new manager with their capital

FOREWORD

I am one of the surviving dinosaurs within the financial services industry. I began my career approximately 50 years ago as a stockbroker and ended it as Chief Executive Officer of UBS Financial Services. Back then, we thrived in an industry that proudly stated we were "bullish on America" or that "everyone listened" when a particular wire house spoke. It was an era of optimism. The very concept of short-selling was relegated to a few hedge funds and traders. Seeking a decline in a listed security was closely considered un-American. Research analysts would opine on a security as to ok to buy, neutral, or ok to sell, never a report that signaled ok to short. In the early days, a "short against the box" was a tactic to lock in a capital gain by shorting an equal amount of shares against a long position.

Today, due to increased volatility, boom and bust bubbles, overpriced story stocks and financial crisis driven by over-leverage, one can make a prudent case that you can protect your portfolio and even seek a profit by engaging in short-selling. The challenge is how to reverse decades of fundamental buy-oriented research into negative fundamental research oriented towards stocks that should decline in value. Fortunately, Portfolio Manager, Nitin K. Sacheti, is providing us with a road map. His book, Downside Protection, which provides us with process and tenets for short-selling in all market environments is a must read for all asset managers, traders, and investors. He shares with us his real-time experiences at Charter Bridge Capital, at Cobalt Capital and at Tiger Europe Management. He currently is managing his own long-short fund, Papyrus Capital. I am a happy investor in his fund.

Now that I have accepted the position of semi-retirement, I have acquiesced to the paradigm shift that has taken place in investing. In today's market environment, you need to hedge with the appropriate portfolio strategy, and you can make money on the downside. My only regret is that I did not have the opportunity of reading Nitin's book prior to 1987, 1998, and in 2008! I would go as far as to suggest to Nitin that his book could also be entitled, "Making Money by Selling Short."

Thank you, Nitin.

Joe Grano

INTRODUCTION

WHY DID I WRITE A BOOK ON

SHORT-SELLING?

I believe a case study approach to learning is valuable because it allows us to supplement our experiences with those of others. I set out to write this book because I hope that my past experience in short-selling, conveyed through cases, combined with the overarching characteristics or 16 tenets I look for in good shorts should help others sharpen their skills, assuming I communicate them properly! However, my book (1) differs from most case-study oriented books while (2) also differing from most short-selling oriented books.

(1) Most case study-oriented books report historical facts in hindsight, after they have occurred. Reporting in hindsight rarely uncovers the steps required to initially identify the situation, a-priori, resulting in an inability to learn from and replicate the process going forward. Instead, I walk through my process of initially discovering a short candidate, the steps taken to determine if it is a good short and the conclusions reached based on the facts obtained. While this results in certain numbers being wrong in hindsight (we

estimate direction, not precision), I think it's a great look at the work involved in assessing a short and the overarching, replicable tenets the reader can utilize to repeat these successful outcomes.

(2) The types of cases I highlight differ from those in most other short-selling oriented books. Many such books tend to entertain with salacious tales of corporate fraud and classics like Enron and WorldCom. While hearing about blow-ups in history and learning about the people involved is fascinating, such shorts are rare, very hard to find (especially a-priori) and often take many years to unravel, so these books do not do a great job of teaching a young analyst how to source and diligence a large quantity of great shorts. I write this book in somewhat of a stream of consciousness to provide the reader with insight into my thoughts as I uncover a different type of short: the singles, doubles and triples that occur regularly and create a high batting average for an entire portfolio rather than a single home-run. I hope this allows the reader to learn my entire short-selling process: the pattern recognition involved in identifying great short candidates and the follow-through work involved in properly conducting diligence to generate an outsized return.

As no single list or perspective is comprehensive, I hope readers will supplement my book with Kathryn Staley's *The Art of Short Selling* and other great investment books to build a toolkit of past experience and patterns likely to repeat themselves in the future through all sorts of cycles.

Short-selling through cycles is not easy, especially over the last 8-10 years. Excessive liquidity has entered equity markets due to an increased supply of money from quantitative easing and a great rotation from bonds to equities as interest rates have declined, favoring passive instead of active investment management. On top of this, limited revenue growth across businesses has increased investor appetite for growth stocks (which are growing revenue), regardless of bottom line earnings growth. Adding to this, low interest rates have caused the return hurdle on capital projects to decline. Businesses have in turn pursued low **IRR** projects (typically the best short-selling candidates) which boost revenue, causing their stock prices to rise (further magnified by passive investing) despite a lack of growth in earnings.

The result of all this has been a very limited ability to use typical short-selling processes to generate returns. Many investors who simply go long stocks with low valuations and short stocks with high valuations have gotten destroyed because earnings are not what the market necessarily looks at today to value companies. For many years, Tesla's stock price has been correlated to the number of cars sold and Netflix's to the number of subscriber additions, regardless of the profitability of those cars or subscribers. As such, just about every short-only fund has closed while returns have been abysmal for most long/short managers relative to the S&P 500.

I've been in the hedge fund business for about 13 years now, so I've seen the 2006-2007 market, the 2008-early 2009 market and the mid 2009-2019 market. This last period of 2009-2019 requires a much more rigorous short-selling framework. Because this environment has been so tough for short-sellers, the silver lining is that when interest rates begin rising again and investors value businesses more fundamentally, the greater market dispersion should make the more rigorous tenets discussed in this book work even more effectively!

Being a good short-seller requires (1) the right framework, (2) some level of judgement, logic, and creativity, and (3) hard work and incredible diligence. I think (1) and (3) are very easily replicable and through this book I hope to walk through (1) in Chapter 1 and (2) in the cases to empower the reader to build his or her short process and use (3) to uncover fertile opportunities. I begin with a brief description of my background in this introduction and discuss how my work experience has shaped my perspective on short-selling. In Chapter 1, I provide a comprehensive list of the process steps I follow and tenets I look for when shorting, and in the following chapters I highlight corresponding case studies on shorts through my career. Finally, I end with short-burst examples of many shorts that passed the initial sourcing phase but failed to fulfill the tenets during the diligence phase, leading me to pass on them.

CAREER BACKGROUND

In 2006, I began my investment management career at Ampere Capital, a spin-off from Ardsley Partners/Moore Capital. I worked for a Portfolio Manager with a phenomenal knack for analyzing businesses in the technology, media, telecommunications and consumer spaces. I first started investing in these sectors, which helped me to fish in the right ponds given the significant creative destruction and dispersion of outcome in these industries. As such, many of the future cases in Chapters 2-9 involved businesses being disintermediated or undergoing innovators' dilemmas in these industries.

In 2010, I joined Tiger Europe Management, a Europe focused investment fund seeded by Julian Robertson's Tiger Management. My time at Tiger allowed me to (1) research more European companies where I realized information is often less likely to be priced-in vs. US competitors, because companies are smaller/traded less, and investment managers are not as focused on deep diligence as their US counterparts. European markets have turned out to be a very fertile places for identifying shorts. Also, (2) Julian Robertson stressed feet-on-the-streets research including attending industry conferences, walking trade-show floors and building a rolodex of industry experts. This focus on uniting the practical with the theoretical permeated to seed funds like Tiger Europe and I significantly improved my 'short-selling game' by adopting this as part of my process.

After Tiger, I worked for Cobalt Capital, managing the firm's investments in the technology, media, telecom and consumer spaces. The Portfolio Manager at Cobalt is a very gifted investor with a great knack for risk management, hence his phenomenal performance in 2008 vs. the indices. From Cobalt, I learned the importance of catalysts on shorts to limit open-ended stock price moves upwards (a concept to which I'll come back).

After Cobalt, I joined Charter Bridge Capital where I was given significant autonomy, allowing me to spend a few years crystallizing all my past experiences into a robust process that works. Upon leaving, the Portfolio Manager and I sorted through the trade sheets and he provided me a letter and track record that showed I was +/- a couple percent each year on my shorts in 2013/2014 (about flat, overall), despite the market up 51%, hence significant alpha generation on my shorts.

Upon leaving Charter Bridge in 2015, I launched my investment fund, Papyrus Capital at the beginning of 2016 to incorporate all of my previous experiences: (1) industry expertise in technology, media, telecom and consumer, (2) a robust rolodex of industry experts, (3) emphasis on the US and Western Europe and (4) catalysts on shorts to properly manage risk. In our first three years of operation, 2016-2018, Papyrus was also about +/- a couple percent in annualized returns on the short side. This performance compares to a 5-year total return of 96.3% for the S&P 500 Total Return Index (14% annualized) (excluding 2015 when setting up Papyrus).

WHY DO I CONSIDER FLAT SHORT RETURNS
WORTHY OF WRITING A BOOK?

I consider this good performance due to the aforementioned lack of dispersion of individual companies and the distortion of fundamentals by Central Bank quantitative easing that has caused seemingly great short candidates to massively outperform. I also believe that breakeven (or slightly losing) short performance in up markets offers a phenomenal insurance policy and combined with positive absolute performance in down markets means overall positive short returns and significant alpha generation over the long run.

Moreover, my process differs from many of the short-sellers often dubbed great by Wall Street in recent years. Many of these, for example, one who shorted a 25% position in Valeant Pharmaceuticals, did copious levels of work and timed a fraud in significant size. The investor made a great return, but I believe this sort of short-selling is one-off and does not lend itself to a high batting average on many names. This strategy represents poor risk management because at some point, despite the levels of work the investor does, he/she risks being early on timing or wrong on a single 25% position and wiping away his/her entire fund with just a tripling or quadrupling of the stock. It's hard for me to believe this strategy will yield the best short returns over time, despite Wall Street celebrity status. My process, as described in this book, is designed to generate a high batting average in an abundance of names to outperform over the long run, which I believe is the best short-selling strategy and also

is the result of a process that can be widely utilized across
many industries and companies.

CHAPTER 1: THE PROCESS AND TENETS OF SHORT-SELLING

1. IDEA SOURCING

The idea sourcing phase is very important. At the top of the funnel, it's very easy to get lost in doing a small amount of research in a lot of companies rather than working mile-wide, inch-deep to find the best opportunities to take into the diligence phase. Following the five Tenets of the Sourcing Process discussed later will help to keep the time in the sourcing phase focused on the most fruitful opportunities.

2. THE DILIGENCE PROCESS

A. Primary Source: Importance of Earnings Transcripts in addition to Filings

When first learning a new business that looks like an interesting short, I start with the primary source documents to build an understanding of the business the way the company hopes to portray itself. While in high school history class, we learned that primary source documents are objective and secondary sources are subjective, anyone who reads a company filing, especially in a potential short-selling candidate, can see that primary source documents are far from objective. However, as per the tenet of empathy discussed later, putting yourself in the shoes of the company allows you to begin thinking like management and understanding their motives and objectives. After beginning with the information, they carefully curate for the SEC in their filings, my second step involves reading company transcripts and investor presentations. Management tends to speak off the cuff when presenting at a conference or in the Q&A of an earnings call. Reading through years of transcripts gives me particular insight into how the company might change its tune which is HUGELY valuable in identifying short candidates. The best shorts tend to be in businesses with bombastic management teams selling a story that often does not materialize, or with management ignoring previous unmet projections and making new, aggressive estimates for the future. Given the sheer number of businesses that investors follow, it's often hard to remember what a particular management team said five years ago in a random investor presentation. At Papyrus Capital, we keep the data handy in Evernote, which allows us to easily categorize and identify changes in management communication. Also, in transcripts, management often mentions certain numbers not found in SEC filings. Going through transcripts and incorporating these quantitative metrics/numbers in an excel-based financial model every few quarters allows us to track changes to the business that sell-side models often miss. For example, in a particular tech short that releases a new product every few years at a higher ASP (average selling price), inputting unit volumes and revenue information from management can allow us to back into the ASP (since exact ASP is usually unknown) and identify its trend over time, giving us a sense of when earnings power might degrade with ASP declines.

B. Talk to Industry Experts, Attend Industry Trade Shows and Canvas Every Industry Related Source You Can Find

A strong cadre of industry experts is one of the most important tools of a good short-seller. As you will likely glean from the book, I believe that short-selling is most fruitful with an in-depth understanding of a business and its structural changes. I can learn a new business quickly when working with a thoughtful industry expert with sound judgement. That helps me ramp faster while focusing on the metrics that matter. Industry experts, also, often help me identify new short-selling candidates since they keep a more mindful eye on changes in their industry while I am busy jumping

from industry to industry. This was especially helpful
in the Imagination (IMG LN) short discussed later. A
rolodex is not the only way to rely on industry experts;
I can often find them through attending trade shows,
walking the floor and talking to anyone who is willing to give me the time of day (Empathy Tenet). On
Wall Street, I most often speak to management teams
who are trained to talk to analysts but when I attend
tradeshows, I often speak to salespeople or product
professionals who are used to discussing all competitive
products with customers. This helps me understand
who else sells a competitive product in a way the CEO
might not communicate. While a CEO knows most of
his prospective investors will not know the list of competitors, a salesperson knows his customers have talk-
ed to all competitors, so he or she is not telling them
anything they don't already know. What lead John
Carreyrou to crack his incredible story on Theranos?
– the multitudes of conversations he had with former
employees manifested the truth.

C. Modeling and Valuation

Modeling the business varies based on the individual
setup, which is part of the art to short-selling – knowing
what info to glean in the industry diligence phase and
accurately estimating how that flows into the overall
financial forecasting of the business. In one situation,

simply modeling price and quantity of a single product company yields a conclusion because most of the work involves industry work to accurately estimate that price and quantity (in the case of the InvenSense (INVN) short). In other cases, such as the Elpida short case, I must model the cost structure of every player in the industry to determine the supply while also modeling demand from every end market to determine supply/demand and the prevailing market price. Modeling should be used to accurately estimate the metrics which Wall Street scrutinizes and short when those turn.

3. SETUP AND CONCLUSION – WHEN TO SHORT

While one can never perfectly time the setup on a short, getting as close as possible reduces volatility and a mark to market (a short-term unrealized) loss while waiting for the thesis to play out. While being a great short-seller requires patience (and patient investors), shorting before a large revenue miss versus consensus helps to get in just before the stock cracks. Properly determining setup and valuation requires the perfect coalescing of industry reading and conversations with a Five Forces framework that yields a significantly variant opinion versus sell-side consensus. This does not happen often and sometimes I am early but combining the process discussed above with the tenets below to result in a breakdown of the metrics at which Wall Street looks can yield a great opportunity, as discussed in our cases.

THE TENETS OF SHORT-SELLING

TENETS OF THE SOURCING PROCESS

1. Follow the Actions of the Industry Leader/100LB Gorilla

The equity market over the last 10 years has been the era of the ecosystem. Industry leaders like Facebook, Google, Amazon, Netflix and Apple have seen incredible appreciation in their stocks (and in most cases, earnings power) as they have built massive ecosystems in which we live our lives, all with little capital invested in the ground. The shift to a knowledge/services economy has enabled growth with a lot less capital expenditure relative to the past. Building Facebook requires much less capital expenditure than railroads, fiber optic networks, and other innovations of the past. As such, today's industry leaders have been able to grow extremely quickly, disintermediating competitors in their wake. Identifying these disintermediated competitors yields an immense short opportunity. Watching the moves of the 100LB gorilla is integral not only for businesses in which secular declines are accelerated based on disintermediation, but also vital for cases where single-product growth companies that were once innovators are disintermediated by a larger and better capitalized competitor. That competitor introduces the same product with the benefit of cheaper production and distribution. Watching the moves of the largest companies in an industry has been one of the most fertile ways for me to source short opportunities.

2. Follow the Actions of Insiders

Insiders know their companies better than anyone else and they will always be incentivized by their self-interest. While we hope that every manager aligns incentives with shareholders as well as the Warren Buffetts of the world, the truth is that the vast majority do not run companies as sound as Berkshire and do not own as much stock as BRK's founders. They run businesses that cater to the quarter and the short-term. They cultivate corporate cultures that value politicking in a quest to get as rich as possible, as quickly as possible, without regard to long-term shareholder value. InsiderScore (incredible resource for identifying insider stock sales) did an analysis in 2012 that looked at 10b5-1 selling plans (automated selling at pre-specified prices and timing) which showed a -3.1% return over a 6-month period on companies where clustered insider selling (multiple insiders) occurred on market caps above $200m (data collected from 2004-2012). As such, following insider selling provides another very fertile ground for hunting for shorts. I run an additional level of screening at Papyrus Capital to identify insider selling that occurs after a stock has dropped 20%+ in a short period of time. Management selling even after a drop in the stock often reveals the first cracks of much more to come. That said, insiders sell for many reasons, so insider sales alone are insufficient evidence to short a stock. Still, the tenet narrows the field where I can then apply the other tenets of our short-selling process.

3. Keep a Close Eye on the IPO Market

While recently discussing the Lyft (ride-sharing company) IPO, Buffett said that he had not participated in an IPO since Ford in 1955. Over the last several decades, the use of the public markets has somewhat shifted. Many years ago, the public market was a tool to access large amounts of capital unavailable in the private markets. As such, growth companies would IPO to raise money. However, as the private markets developed, the amount of capital a company could raise in the private markets matched that of the public markets. Accordingly, private companies often seek the IPO market, not to raise capital, but to sell shares to public market investors. Many companies that have hit a peak in growth will IPO for exactly this purpose, which fits well with our selling shareholder tenet, above. Taking this thought process one step further, many of the founders of these companies attempt to maximize their net worth by timing the IPO 6-24 months before growth peaks. They often do this by initially selling a small number of shares in the IPO (so that the float is low and supply/demand of stock work in their favor), then posting a few quarters of 'beats' of sell-side consensus which often causes new momentum-oriented investors to push their stock price up on the back of a small float. After a few quarters of this, IPO lockups (where management and other founders are restricted from selling stock) often expire 180 and 360 days (multiple tranches) after the IPO and founding shareholders can sell into a peak stock price. Keeping a mindful eye on these dynamics often allows me to identify shorts right as their growth stories unravel, proving very profitable at the right time.

4. Put Yourself Out There: Empathy

While a bit tongue-in-cheek and more apt for dating, putting yourself out there as a short-selling tenet for sourcing means all sorts of things – read the Economist weekly and think through the changing world, go to retail stores and notice shifting trends, build relationships with people across different industries and talk to them about what they see, attend trade shows in different sectors and walk the floors, read books about all different industries and people. All of this helps to put yourself in the shoes of others which is ultimately the most important quality of a short-seller: empathy. Think like a competitor who wants to get into a new space; what will he/she do to create a better product? Think like a purchaser who knows he/she is getting squeezed: how long before he/she identifies another supplier? Think like a consumer moving from a fad to a competitor: how does he/

she manifest his/her changing tastes? I put myself in the minds of decision-makers to identify and conduct diligence on great short opportunities.

5. Look for Innovators' Dilemma Shorts – High Multiple on Peak Earnings

I believe innovators' dilemma shorts at high multiples on peak earnings are the best type of shorts. While secularly declining shorts are great, their declines are often priced into consensus estimates for future earnings declines and in low earnings multiples. You must get the timing really right in secularly declining shorts. Otherwise, if the tail is slightly longer than the market anticipates and the company beats estimates, the multiple and earnings likely both get adjusted upwards and the stock massively rallies. The benefit of innovators' dilemma shorts is that they are often the first mover in a fast-growing industry. Usually, having recently gone public, they trade at a high valuation on earnings that sell-side brokers predict will continue to grow at very fast rates. In other words, I am shorting the business at a peak multiple on extremely high future earnings estimates. This gives me the opportunity to short a decline in earnings along with a decline in the multiple, which provides a phenomenal margin of safety on a short since it is priced for perfection. If I can assess any of the tenets below, increased competition, low switching costs, poor placement on the cost curve, value destructive unit economics...etc, I can short and make a hefty profit!

TENETS OF THE DILIGENCE PROCESS

1. Utilize Porter's Five Forces in Short-Selling

Michael Porter's Five Forces framework is extremely helpful in identifying great short candidates and many of the short tenets that follow are incorporated into the Five Forces analysis. Like any checklist, using the Five Forces builds the basis for questions in my fact-finding endeavor, helping me ask industry insiders the right questions and short when fundamentals break down. While signs from the Five Forces occur every step of the way, we should be mindful for negative signs in the primary source phase because it's often listed in company filings while centering questions in the diligence phase that solve for them.

2. Understand the Cost Curve and Identify the High Cost Producer

Also, very important to any business case, long or short, is understanding where the company lies on the industry cost curve. The lowest cost producer in any industry pretty much always fares the best unless the industry entirely dissolves. In periods of boom, most investors do not differentiate between the highest and lowest cost producers as rising tides lift all ships but when demand drops, the worst producers are exposed, offering short-sellers ripe pickings. Assessing the cost curve of incremental supply also proves fruitful in short-selling – if an innovator designs a novel product but is subscale, once a legacy player can replicate the product at a lower cost of production/distribution, the legacy player can steal market share from the innovator, rendering the innovator a great short candidate. While placement on the cost curve seems obvious, actually identifying it is much tougher. The cases in future chapters will identify the steps required to uncover positions along a cost curve.

3. Look for Near-Term Maturities

Near term debt maturities (and their interest rates) can help to catalyze a short thesis just as much as a new competitor, especially in highest cost producers in industries entering a downturn. While refinancing has been very easy over the last ten years through QE, as tapering ensues, balance sheet risks will become a much more actionable short tenet.

4. Understand the Unit Economics to Assess Value Destruction

My greatest takeaway from any Economics class came from my AP Economics teacher at Loomis Chaffee (who also taught Henry Kravis). He gave us an example of a wooden vulture business. If I were the manufacturer of wooden vultures and it cost me $30 in materials to make an ugly wooden vulture that someone would buy from me for only $25, I'd be destroying value. Odds are, unless I get some incredible personal benefit from making wooden vultures and I'm economically irrational, I won't continue to make wooden vultures. This sounds obvious but there are countless examples of public companies in which management highlights revenue growth, new products, and industry buzzwords (like big data or AI or data science) but the simple unit economics are value destructive. Assessing the very simple step of unit economics yields a great understanding of a business's longer term earnings power: what's the price of the product, what does it cost, how much does it cost to market to the subscriber and what are the ongoing costs to keep running the plant? For example, we estimate that Stitch Fix, an online personal shopping platform spends more on marketing to acquire a new customer than that customer generates in cash flow over his/her (very short) life. While revenue grows with each new customer, we believe the unit economics of this business are value destructive.

5. Identify Increasing Competition

A changing competitive landscape is one of the most important metrics to look for when short-selling and often manifests itself in the industry analysis phase. While it seems simple based on an understanding of elementary microeconomics, identifying actual competition is a lot tougher in the real world. Some competitors are quick to communicate new product launches to Wall Street or their customers but slow to implement them. Moreover, with the sheer increase in number of short-sellers over the last several years, short theses that aggrandize impending competition tend to get disseminated publicly, bringing in trading-oriented short-sellers who do not dig as deeply as I do. While this might have a short-term impact on the company based on supply/demand dynamics around the stock (more short-sellers creating downward pressure), I have learned that it's imperative not to get carried away by small stock price moves based on theoretical competition. You should only short when you see the competition in the market, not when it seems like it might come. The former results in structural earnings power declines, a shortable case with high conviction. The theoretical increase in competition may cause a small drop in the stock but is meaningless in the future if the competition does not enter the space and may result in a violent squeeze up in the stock as the shorter-term short-sellers run for the exits. This is one of the most valuable lessons in this book for a high batting average on shorts, so, please, be patient and short only when competition comes.

6. Identify Businesses with Low Switching Costs

Related to the competition point above, high switching costs are also paramount to a great short case. It's much easier to short a B2B supplier of components to an Apple iPhone than it is to short a consumer company with a great brand, even if both have a better, new competitor in the market. Apple cares only about price and quality of a component and will switch to a new competitor almost instantaneously while a consumer or bureaucratic company will be much slower to change since you don't get fired for buying IBM or Cisco. This tenet also speaks to the aforementioned tenets around (1) watching the moves of the 100LB gorilla/industry leader and how they change their buying patterns and (2) empathy, always putting yourself in the shoes of the customer. I know how Apple thinks and how quickly they make decisions and can bet accordingly. I also know how the consumer thinks if I can put myself in his/her shoes and can understand his/her switching cost rationale.

7. Do Not Short a Product Customers Love

Complementary to the switching costs and competition tenets, do not short a stock where customer calls reveal a love for the product. In such cases, especially in B2B products where customers tend to be less emotional than individual consumers, comparable products usually don't compare, and the product clearly adds significant value to the customers. Related to competition, I did not short Tesla until far superior electric cars from Jaguar, Hyundai, Audi and Porsche entered the market. Before 2019, the Model S, in my opinion, was the best car out there and customers loved it.

8. Short When the Industry View Vastly Differs from Wall Street's View

As you'll reader in numerous examples, when Wall Street's near-term view differs vastly from industry experts, that's often the best time to short since Wall Street will likely change its tune after the industry view is manifested in the numbers. The point where Wall Street is still optimistic and the industry is extremely pessimistic offers a pretty spectacular a-ha moment, at which shorting is usually very satisfying! For example, in Chapter 2, when industry experts painted a vastly different picture of INVN's proprietary manufacturing process becoming a cost rather than a benefit versus competitors' manufacturing processes, I knew it was the right time to short!

9. Do Not Short Solely on Valuation; Short Based on Wall Street Metrics Breaking Down

As we build our business mosaic and get closer to developing a conclusion on a short, determining the metrics Wall Street focuses on is so important in shorting in a rising, QE-fueled market. Many investors, historically, have shorted based on accounting red flags or lack of earnings generation or valuation. While these are clearly the hallmarks of bad businesses, such red flags can go unnoticed for a very, very long time if they do not create insolvency risk because Wall Street just doesn't focus on them. Instead, my experience has taught me that you make the most money in the shortest timeframe with the least risk when shorting businesses where the metrics Wall Street focuses on are inflecting downward. For example, in the case of our short in FIO (Chapter 4), Wall Street focuses solely on revenue and gross margins each quarter. The company could spend oodles on opex and not generate any earnings, but no one would care (within reason) as long as they continued to beat estimates on revenue and gross margin. Our analysis involved determining when pricing declined due to increased competition and revenue growth slowed while gross margins dropped. That was the time to short FIO. I hope you understand the importance of this tenet, best understood in practice, through the cases in the rest of the book.

10. Stick to What is Predictable/Feels Right – We Don't Get Paid Extra for Forcing an Idea

When concluding that a short-selling candidate looks ripe to short, just as important as empathy is assessing conviction levels and commitment/consistency biases. When doing a lot of work on a name, we are often tricked into assuming that it is therefore a good short. Because we don't want to admit the last 30-50 hours were wasted, we might stretch the truth in our mind to fit our tenets. However, it's important to stay as intellectually honest as possible and make sure that every-thing we learned and believe about the future prospects of the business are within our ability to predict. We do not get paid extra for forcing opinions where we do not have enough information to predict the future or where we have so much information that we cannot isolate the signal from the noise to develop a predictable conclusion. Knowing what we know and what we don't know and acting based on what we know is so important for our batting average.

11. Short in Size Small and Other
Technical Considerations

As Keynes has remarked, "the market can stay irrational a lot longer than you can stay solvent." This statement holds true but on steroids for short-selling. While one might ultimately be proven right on a short over the long run, in the short run, should a stock double, triple or quadruple in one's face, the position size increases with open-ended losses. Now, multiply that by 40-50 shorts that your average long/short equity hedge fund runs and think about the permanent capital risk. At Papyrus Capital, each short is about 0.50% to 1.5% of the total capital base ensuring that we can withstand volatility when competition takes a bit longer than expected or the capital markets stay open longer for a business with near-term maturities or a new product gets introduced that keeps earnings higher for longer. Even if I believe the ultimate earnings power may decline, sizing small keeps time on my side. Cost and availability of borrow are also considerations, like any other hurdle in a short (similar to a dividend yield) though borrow costs are fluid and what might look expensive one day may change the next. For example, I was short **GPRO** with a 90% cost to borrow in 2014 just before the expiration of management's lockup. The increased supply of stock onto the market caused both the borrow cost and the stock to drop, hence, sometimes, it's beneficial to short a high borrow cost if it's changing quickly.

CHAPTER 2: INVENSENSE

SHORTING A PREVIOUSLY ADVANTAGEOUS
MANUFACTURING PROCESS THAT BECAME A
DISADVANTAGE

INTRODUCTION

InvenSense (INVN) is a producer of gyroscopes and accelerometers used to measure motion in smartphones, tablets and gaming consoles. Most simplistically, an accelerometer moves along an X-Y axis to determine when a phone is horizontal or vertical so that it can automatically shift between landscape and portrait. The gyroscope contains a small ball that moves along the X-Y-Z plane, measuring side-to-side movement like the accelerometer, but also tracking three-dimensional motion by including depth on the Z axis. When you play a video game on your phone, the gyroscope allows your phone to know that you move the device up/down/to the side or along an arc.

In a typical gyroscope, a ball moves around in a non-pressurized chamber (a MEMS or micro-electro-mechanical system). The chamber tracks movements and transmits the information to an ASIC (application specific integrated circuit, i.e. semiconductor chip). The ASIC calculates the movements and transmits the information to the apps processor (brains) of the phone. In a generic gyroscope design, the information is transmitted from the MEMS to the ASIC through a conductive metal wire.

INVN patented a gyroscope that instead transmits information from the MEMS to the ASIC through a conductive layer that is also the wall around the ball's chamber. The gyroscope is made using a process entitled the Nasiri Fabrication Process after the founder of the company. The Nasiri Fabrication Process allowed INVN to seal the MEMS that holds the ball using an aluminum germanium bonding method. That seal serves as the conductive layer to transmit information from the MEMS to the ASIC, replacing the generic conductive wire between the two parts. The Nasiri Process allows the ASIC to fit right on top of the MEMS, eliminating the need for the conductive wire and space in-between the MEMS and the ASIC, and therefore reducing the amount of silicon needed for the device. The Nasiri Process enabled INVN to produce at a lower cost and make a product small enough for a smartphone. As such, INVN's sales into the smartphone/tablet/gaming sectors exploded and the company IPO'ed in late 2011.

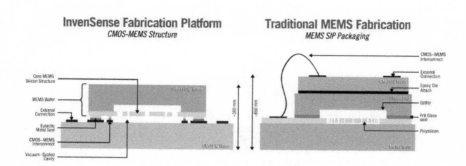

IDEA SOURCING

I came across INVN in 2011 over the course of my regular IPO monitoring (IPO Monitoring Tenet) and read the company prospectus. Though I didn't see any additional competition and the company's manufacturing process seemed innovative, the business proved interesting because it was a single product company with a very high gross margin for the semiconductor space (potential Innovators' Dilemma Tenet). I came back to INVN in early 2013 on the advice of a friend and after noticing a large increase in insider sales by management (Follow Insider Actions Tenet).

Two characteristics of INVN made it a good short candidate: insider action, and, most critically, increasing competition. It was particularly interesting that a jump in the stock in the Spring of 2013 caused new 10-b5 plans to be triggered by executives who already had existing plans in place, therefore accelerating their stock sales. Coupled with this, when I google searched for mobile phone gyroscopes, my search yielded more competitors vs. in late 2011. As such, I began the diligence phase of filings/transcripts/

sell-side research, industry whitepapers and conversations with experts.

DILIGENCE

Industry whitepapers and conversations with experts in the space revealed two threats to INVN. First, a change in manufacturing technology enabled other players to catch up to INVN with smaller and lower cost products. The Nasiri Fabrication Process, resultingly, was hitting a technological wall. Second, some of the functionality of the battery-intensive gyroscope was replaced by a newly designed sensor-hub.

As discussed above, the value of the Nasiri Fabrication Process is the ability to use the walls around the MEMS as a conductivity mechanism while using the MEMS as the base of the package (accelerometer/gyroscope combined chip, called a 6-axis chip) and the ASIC as the top, thereby reducing the overall size vs. stacking one on top of the other with wires in between. In the Nasiri Process, the MEMS and the ASIC need to be the same size because they form the top and bottom of the package (with the gyroscope and accelerometer in between). Moore's Law, however, dictates that as the ASIC production moves to a smaller semiconductor manufacturing node, the size and cost of the ASIC declines. While INVN's 6-axis product (accelerometer/ gyroscope combination) was at a size of 3x3mm, new competitors could manufacture their ASICs at 2.5mm. This was a huge advantage for new competitors because a smaller ASIC could mean a lower cost while INVN was limited by their ability to reduce the size of the MEMS. The MEMS, unlike the ASIC, was not subject to Moore's Law because its size is limited by the moving ball for the gyroscope, which requires a certain amount of weight. In the Nasiri Process, the ball limited both the MEMS and the ASIC, rather than just the MEMS because the two were the floor and ceiling of the chamber; the Nasiri Process combined the accelerometer and the gyroscope into that single chamber. The more generic TSV method used by competitors separated the accelerometer and gyroscope and stacked them so the overall chip could be reduced to 2.5x2.5mm because the accelerometer did not need to be located next to the gyroscope, further reducing costs versus the Nasiri process. For example, if my living room (gyroscope) and kitchen (accelerometer) are next to each other, my floor and ceiling must be wider. If I put my living room on top of my kitchen, the floor and ceiling can be narrower. On top of all of this, Moore's Law resulted in smaller and smaller wires needed to connect the MEMS and ASIC in the generic process, reducing the height disadvantage vs. the Nasiri process. The shift from advantage to disadvantage of the Nasiri Process was the lynchpin in the case that made INVN a great short, especially given lofty sell-side expectations and almost no sell-side knowledge of the obsolescence here and what it would do to INVN's revenue, margins and earnings (Innovators' Dilemma and Industry Differs from Wall Street View Tenet).

A few competitors pioneered and took advantage of the improved efficiency in manufacturing and design. Maxim purchased a company called Sensor Dynamic, which gave them a gyroscope, and they launched a 3-axis discrete gyroscope in 2012, with a 6-axis 3x3mm size product to be launched in 2013. Freescale, an additional competitor, was launching a 6-axis product likely in early 2014. Kionix, a subsidiary of Rohm, developed an even more efficient and inexpensive product, combining an accelerometer with a compass to use the Earth's pole as a proxy for a gyroscope. At a price point of $0.50 relative to $1.50, the product undercut a typical 6-axis gyroscope. Though it was an inferior product, it proved great for the low-end demand in China.

Through my conversations, I learned that INVN was not only facing competition on the fabrication process, but also from a new smartphone component that would make some of the discrete 6-axis accelerometer/gyroscope's functions obsolete. The gyroscope is extremely battery intensive. It's always moving, always on, and relies on the phone's apps processor, significantly draining the phone's battery. Samsung was pushing the integration of the power source of the phone's many sensors, including the gyroscope, into one sensor hub. The sensor hub would be a separate MCU (essentially, smaller apps processor), which would power all the sensors on the phone at once. The gyroscope/accelerometer ASIC itself, then, would have a decreased functionality, as some of the functions would be shifted to the sensor hub, further decreasing its value.

I learned that the lower manufacturing costs from reduction in ASIC size and sensor hub attracted larger, better capitalized competitors with bigger distribution networks and a lower cost structure into the sector, further confirming an innovators' dilemma short with a poor position on the industry cost curve tenet.

Bosch, a large German engineering and electronics company, never expected a gyroscope to be used in a smartphone, so the company was surprised that Apple introduced one in the iPhone 4 at a $1.50 price point, allowing INVN and STM to garner 50% gross margins. In response, Bosch built a 6-axis product at 3x3mm that sampled with customers in early 2013. Bosch targeted 10% market share by Q4 2013, with most of that taken from INVN. The company also thought it could get a 2x2mm product out by 2015 based on clever stacking. Bosch was a lower cost operator than INVN because it owned its production facilities (Industry Cost Curve Tenet) rather than outsourcing manufacturing.

ST Micro (STM) had long been in the industry and their 6-axis product was the highest gross margin product for the entire company. Like Bosch, it had its own manufacturing facilities, so it produced at a lower cost than INVN. However, the real cost advantage did not come until the generic process became cheaper than the Nasiri Fabrication Process.

Through all of my conversations with experts in the field, I found that the 2012/early 2013 price of $1.50 per gyroscope was unlikely to hold given the new competition at smaller sizes and costs and the transition to the sensor hub. By the end of 2013, prices would compress to $0.90-$1.00, and would continue to drop in 2014/2015.

Sell-side Conversations – the most fascinating part of a great short is the divergence between the thoughts of industry experts and sell-side analysts (Industry Differs from Wall Street View Tenet). As discussed in Chapter 1, sell-side analysts are often paid by the company through banking business to maintain a positive view of the company and you can also bet that very few, if any, sell-side analysts have conversations and attend industry conferences at the same depth as capable short-sellers. Wall Street and Industry diverged on the following points:

- Sell-side: Expect INVN to win Apple as a customer (they were currently using STM) at a higher ASP and margin than INVN's corporate average. My thought: I know Apple NEVER pays market price for any component. They always beat up their suppliers.

- Sell-side: INVN has a lower cost structure due to the Nasiri Process. My thought: This was now a stale fact given the technology changes dictated by Moore's Law.

- Sell-side: INVN has always been the first in the industry to get smaller and will continue to do so based on a better process. My thought: See above!

- Sell-side: Bosch is not focused on the mobile market. Its focus has shifted to the wearables market and auto. My thought: I spoke to Bosch and this was totally incorrect.

FRAMING THE BULL CASE

An investment bank initiated coverage on INVN in mid-2014 with a $21 price target based on 22x CY2015 EPS of $0.88 plus $1.21 in cash per share. The report claimed INVN was first mover with the manufacturing advantage of the Nasiri Process that allowed the company to eliminate several manufacturing steps and continue to innovate by putting more and more sensors on a single chip. Clearly, my research told me otherwise!

VALUATION AND MODELING

Based on my industry diligence, I looked at assessing earnings power by FY16 (3/2016) to determine my assessment for INVN vs. the sell-side consensus. I assumed that by FY16, prices could drop to the $0.70-0.75 range and I gave INVN credit for doubling units vs. FY14 given a higher gyroscope attach rate (the percentage of phones with gyroscopes) and new internet-of-things products, like FitBits, that might also utilize gyroscopes/accelerometers. Those price and quantity assumptions resulted in an estimated revenue of about $400m but much lower gross margins of the low 40s% vs. mid 50s% at the time of research. This was because prices of gyroscopes were likely to go down faster than the cost to make them, resulting in margin compression. These assumptions suggested gross profit only marginally above operating expenditures, proving that like so many other single-trick, innovators' dilemma shorts, once prices dropped due to competition, a single product company could not sustain its operating costs, i.e. became a sub-scale, high cost producer incapable of earning a profit.

SETUP AND CONCLUSION

When it looked like INVN was about to break in mid-2013, I shorted the stock in the high teens.

In October 2013, the stock rallied to $20 based on the expectation that INVN gyroscopes were designed into the iPhone 5S. I acknowledged the possibility and knew it would cause noise in the stock because the market considers the iPhone and its components the best products in the space. As the INVN product became commoditized, however, it could only be competitive for an iPhone design based on pricing/gross margins lower than their corporate average, so I remained short despite the rally in the stock. That said, I found out about a month later that they were not in the iPhone 5S.

In March 2014, Apple rumors swirled again that INVN had won the contract for the iPhone 6, causing the stock to rally to $22. I again stuck with my original analysis on the short case. In July 2014, INVN further rallied to $24 based on a revenue beat on CQ2 earnings and steady gross margins. Meanwhile, my checks showed pricing continuing to decline so it was only a matter of time, in my opinion, before INVN began ceding share to competitors with cheaper products.

In September 2014, INVN finally began to crack, dropping to $19 after teardowns of the iPhone 6 revealed that INVN had won the design for a 6-axis gyroscope/accelerometer, but the new iPhone also included a separate accelerometer from Bosch, likely connected to a sensor hub.

In October 2014, INVN finally began to show signs of satisfying my investment thesis as it guided to CQ4 2014 revenue of $108-115m with gross margins in the 46-47% vs. historical gross margins of 50%+ and EPS of $0.17-0.21 vs. sell-side consensus expectations of $0.30. I believed that INVN was clearly starting to see pricing pressure from competitors and had to lower prices to win the Apple business. The stock fell to ~$14 over the following month, though I believed there was much more to come.

In August 2015, INVN reported CQ3 2015 revenue of $106-114m vs. consensus of $116m and gross margins of 44-45%, another step down from the previous year's mid 40s% and 2013's 50% margins, resulting in earnings expectations in the quarter of $0.13-0.15 vs. the street at $0.17. The stock continued to drop into the high single digits by the end of 2015/early 2016 with revenue and margins continuing to drop, limiting the company's earnings power just as I had estimated in 2013.

TENETS MANIFESTED IN INVN

A variety of tenets proved integral in the INVN short. During the idea sourcing phase, I first discovered INVN by following IPOs in 2011. I returned to the stock in 2013 upon noticing insider action. In 2013, the diligence phase of talking to experts revealed that INVN faced increasing competition and there was disagreement between the industry view and Wall Street view, especially around INVN's place on the industry cost curve. My valuation and modeling work also confirmed that the Wall Street assumptions were overly optimistic, and I shorted when Wall Street metrics began breaking down.

I chose to include INVN in this book because, while similar to a couple other shorts, notably FIO (discussed later), it shows us that this pattern occurs repeatedly in tech. Also, the hard part lies in doing the work to learn the business and the technology to determine whether it fits our tenets to short. While the framework and pattern are the exact same between INVN and FIO, the work involved in learning the product is very different.

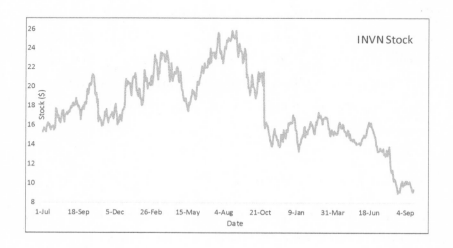

CHAPTER 3: GLOBALSTAR

SHORTING A SEEMINGLY FAVORABLE REGULATORY OUTCOME THAT ACTUALLY IMPAIRS VALUE

INTRODUCTION

Globalstar (GSAT) provides phone and other communications services through a network of satellites in the sky. If you are in a remote area of the world such as Antarctica, you might buy a GSAT satellite phone and subscribe to a GSAT service plan to talk to the rest of the world.

While GSAT primarily generates revenue from its satellite communications service, its conversion of satellite spectrum to terrestrial (wireless) spectrum has driven its market capitalization and stock price over the past several years. Spectrum is the medium by which our phones talk to cell phone towers (terrestrial spectrum), satellites talk to satellite dishes (satellite spectrum) and phones/tablets/computers talk to our wifi router (wifi spectrum) – all expressed in frequency (hertz, Hz). With the advent of smartphones, demand has increased for terrestrial spectrum since additional spectrum is proportional to faster speeds and greater data throughput. For example, if Verizon doubles the spectrum for my city, my download speeds will double. As you can imagine, we consume more data each day, increasing the demand for spectrum (and therefore, the price Verizon/AT&T/T-Mobile are willing to pay for spectrum) so that they can give us greater speeds and more throughput. The increase in data demand has increased the value of terrestrial spectrum and driven a reallocation of spectrum from satellite to terrestrial. In the US, however, the conversion requires Federal Communications Commission (FCC) approval, a process which necessitates that there are no technical risks involved in the change. Because satellite spectrum is most often used in rural areas while terrestrial is most often used in a city, converting satellite to terrestrial spectrum may interfere with other uses of the spectrum in a city and cause disruption of those services. This is what the FCC monitors for in the approval process.

IDEA SOURCING

I was first involved with GSAT in 2013 when reading about different businesses with spectrum holdings. I have been a spectrum bull for many years because I believe data growth should increase spectrum prices, as previously discussed.

In 2013/2014, GSAT proposed to the FCC creating a new, private wifi spectrum channel by combining 11.5 megahertz (MHz) of its own satellite spectrum with 10.5MHz of a neighboring wifi spectrum. Currently, all wifi spectrum is open for public use. That is, any of us can plug a wifi router into a wall and access it through our phones and wifi spectrum, so GSAT's wifi channel would be the only private one. All terrestrial and satellite spectrum bands, however, are private (i.e. AT&T owns some bands that only its customers can use while Verizon owns other bands for its own customers). GSAT could sell or lease its proposed private wifi channel to customers like Amazon who might use the lower-traffic private wifi band to increase internet speeds for its Prime customers, for example. The adjoining wifi band GSAT intended to use, however, was also used by some Bluetooth applications. As a result, the Bluetooth lobbying groups and sellers of Bluetooth applications and devices pushed hard against the proposal and the FCC ruled against GSAT.

GSAT subsequently revised its proposal to the FCC to use only their own 11.5MHz of spectrum (not the 10.5MHz of neighboring wifi spectrum) and to do so at a very low power level of 4 watts to ensure their spectrum would not interfere with neighboring Bluetooth. On December 22, 2016, GSAT received approval of their revised proposal and the stock rallied from $1.47 on 12/20/2016 to $1.84 on 12/23/2016 (+25%). I revisited GSAT after seeing that the revised proposal significantly impaired the value of the spectrum vs. the earlier proposal, making the rise in the stock unwarranted.

Any time a business changes so significantly, it's worth better understanding how the changing business value may impact the longer-term earnings power and net asset value of the company. While the stock price rallied only 25%, the amount of spectrum they would be awarded dropped by almost half and the power level declined significantly. In this case, having had some familiarity with GSAT from 2013, I set out to better understand how the company's monetization characteristics and total addressable market might change. Moreover, with debt coming due soon (Near-Term Maturities Tenet), onerous covenants/leverage might magnify any structural impairments to the business from the revised proposal.

DILIGENCE

In any short, part of my diligence process involves understanding and vetting the company's message and the bull case on the stock (primary source process). In the case of GSAT, the company communicated to investors that the revised FCC approval would allow them to pursue a lease or sale of their spectrum by a wireless operator intending to deploy it for a small cell network. Small cells are smaller wireless towers that might sit on a lamppost in a city or on top of a stadium during a game. They allow the re-use of wireless spectrum, which increases speeds. What does re-use mean? Think about the case of a wifi router; currently, I am in my home and my computer is connected to my wifi router, receiving data at a speed of 50Mbps. You are likely in your home or office, also connected to your wifi router, possibly at a speed similar to mine. Maybe there are 100 more people on your block all in their homes/offices connected to the exact same spectrum at the exact same speeds. However, if all 102 of us were in my home, connecting to my router with the same spectrum, our speeds would be drastically lower. Rather, each of us offloads data onto our own hard-wired connections – we connect to different router antennas, which connect to different hardwired ethernet connections/wifi routers to call up data. Thus, we use the same spectrum without slowing each other down. Similarly, small cells hung on lampposts across the city allow mobile phone users to connect to each lamppost, so they can use the same spectrum without degrading each other's signals. If all the people on a block were using the same spectrum and connecting to a larger wireless tower 3 miles away, the speed would be degraded. GSAT contended that carriers would buy their spectrum to host these small cells that increase the speed of connection. Because small cells operate at lower power levels than wireless towers, the lower power restrictions on GSAT's spectrum would not inhibit them, offering GSAT a market monetization mechanism.

Knowing the changes in the FCC proposal and the company's bull case, I began the reading and fact finding mission discussed in just about every case-related chapter in this book to determine fair value for GSAT.

I spoke with CommScope (a wireless equipment manufacturer), Dish Networks/EchoStar (satellite/wireless businesses), Qualcomm engineers, cable companies, wireless chip manufacturers and resellers, mobile engineers at the consumer electronics show and multiple wireless industry conferences and many more (tenets of empathy, industry discussions). All lead me to a similar set of facts and pointed to a significant impairment of GSAT's spectrum value: The demands of 5G, the newest standard of wireless networks, were incompatible with the small width of the spectrum GSAT had available.

5G (as of 2019, we are on 4G), to be deployed in 2020+, will increase the speed (number of bits per second) our phone will gain from each hertz of spectrum, thereby increasing over-all throughput/efficiency of spectrum and enabling faster broadband speeds (spectral efficiency). With better spectral efficiency, wireless providers will densify their networks by deploying small cells for the reasons discussed above, but not using the spectrum that GSAT offers.

The greater spectral efficiency of 5G comes from wider spectrum channels. 5G channels are 100 MHz wide at 10bits/Hz, as opposed to 4G channels which are 10-20Mhz wide at approximately 4bits/Hz. The speed of our phone is the product of the width of the spectrum channel and the bits/Hz at that width, so speeds in 5G are up to 1,000Mb/second (100MHz*10bits/Hz) compared to up to 80Mb/second (20MHz*4bits/Hz) for 4G. The greater width neces-sary for 5G channels, however, incentivizes carriers to buy spectrum in 100MHz blocks so that it can be deployed as a single channel. Recall that GSAT has only 11.5MHz. Think of a pipe; if I aim to get as much water through a pipe as possible, I will buy a 100ft (in this case MHz) wide pipe, not an 11.5ft wide pipe. Furthermore, most spectrum channels require a guard band on either side (like the steel case of the pipe), so the spectrum does not interfere with what's adjacent. Though GSAT claims they can fit a guard band of 1MHz, just about everyone else knowledgeable about the topic in my conversations has suggested guard bands are 3-5MHz, meaning the effective width of GSAT's spectrum is even smaller than 11.5MHz.

I believed a carrier has little reason to buy this since it would allow them to deploy ~115Mbps (10bits/Hz*11.5MHz), a much slower connection than 1,000Mbps or 1Gbps. While carriers can combine different bands, it's inefficient to do so because the amount of power usage in a phone is a function of the number of channels accessed rather than the width of the channels. In a conversation with Nokia, I learned that while Nokia had achieved high speeds of 3-4Gbps by combining 10 different channels in the lab for a total of 200 MHz of spectrum, the power usage was too great. If a carrier looks to combine two different channels (or two pipes of water), you can bet they will combine two 100MHz channels to get the highest data speeds, not a 100MHz channel and an 11.5MHz GSAT channel.

In my opinion, the limited speed benefit and the disadvantage of power usage significantly reduces the number of buyers of GSAT's spectrum. GSAT's FCC-imposed power restrictions further reduce the buyer pool. The typical metro cell has a power level of 5 watts (above GSAT's 4 watt limit) and a propagation range of about 1000 ft. GSAT's power limitations would prevent carriers from deploying the spectrum on a typical metro tower, so the carrier would be limited to very small 300-400 foot radius pico cells, lacking the flexibility of alternative options.

FRAMING THE BULL CASE

The bulls counter that the demand for spectrum will be so high that companies will be willing to buy even these smaller channels once the large ones are used up, but the disadvantages of GSAT's spectrum are very strong. The wireless carriers are likely to re-use significant swaths of spectrum from other sources and deploy on small cells instead of occupying a whole channel (which should be used for 100Mhz) on a small 11.5MHz swath of GSAT spectrum that can be used only in a few select locations. Sources other than GSAT are widely available: carriers can transition the 135MHz of spectrum they deployed in 2G/3G and buy from a variety of sources. An additional 600MHz of spectrum would be auctioned in 2017, 100MHz would likely be sold by Dish Networks, 150MHz of CBRS spectrum auctioned in 2018/2019, and even more spectrum would be freed up from satellite usage and auctioned by the FCC in the future.

My conversations made me conclude that given the sub-scale, orphaned, power restricted nature of GSAT's spectrum, the wireless chip companies would not likely incorporate the frequency into the antennas for smartphones. It is more important to incorporate the types of spectrum that have a higher likelihood of being deployed, leaving GSAT's frequencies at a low priority. This would be a huge chicken and egg problem for GSAT because no one would buy their spectrum if it were not in an antenna and no antenna company would pay enough attention to GSAT to incorporate it.

All of the above lead me to believe that a sale or lease of GSAT's spectrum in the near-term or long term would be very unlikely. Convinced that GSAT would not likely monetize its spectrum, especially in the near future, I turned to their balance sheet constraints as the next set of catalysts to push the stock down to my assessment of fair value.

VALUATION AND MODELING

I estimated GSAT would generate $20m of EBITDA in 2016 and $8-10m in operating cash flow while spending $25m on capital expenditures. I generously estimated breakeven free cash flow in 2017. They would have liquidity of $20-25m in 2016, between cash and a revolver. However, their contractual obligations, interest payments and principal repayments over the following couple years was many multiples of their liquidity. They would also likely breach covenants in the near-term based on limited EBITDA and free cash flow growth, hence a large cash shortfall and almost zero value to the equity.

SETUP AND CONCLUSION

I shorted GSAT at the end of 2016, soon after the FCC ruling and continued to add to the short as additional datapoints confirmed the short thesis.

In May 2017, the press speculated that GSAT had hired bankers to find a buyer for the business, intending to sell to a wireless or cable company. I viewed the announcement as an attempt to spur an increase in the equity value in order to issue more equity given constraints on a French export credit agency debt (COFACE facility) coming due. I used the opportunity to short more GSAT stock on the heels of a large amount of their debt ($159m) coming due on 6/30/2017.

In early July 2017, GSAT announced an amendment to the COFACE credit facility given the debt that had come due at the time. The Chairman of GSAT funded $33m of the $159m coming due through a common stock offering at $1.85/share. While one could see this as an insider purchase, the Chairman was extremely wealthy and I viewed this as an attempt to stave off the bankruptcy risk by investing a very small percentage of his net worth to keep the business alive in hopes of finding a buyer for the spectrum or the whole company. They also pushed out the additional $144m of the $159m due to be repaid 10/31/2017. The onerous covenants in the credit facility also got pushed out one year (for example, they had to be generating $130m in EBITDA by 2022 vs. $26m in 2017) and they were required to use any spectrum-related lease or sale payments to pay down debt, so equity holders would not see any of this cash flow. I believed the company was kicking the can down the road and postponing the inevitable, given their failure in the past seven months to find a buyer for the company or their spectrum.

Another fascinating part of this credit facility amendment was that the lender required GSAT to update them monthly on the sale process: "No later than the last day of each Month, a report prepared by the Borrower and certified by a Responsible Officer with respect to the business of the Group including (but not limited to) details of the following matters: an update to the then applicable Spectrum Plan including any Spectrum Sale or proposed monetization of the Group's Spectrum rights (including an update and commentary on any relevant process and any key events that have either occurred or are scheduled to occur) together with updated detail on any Spectrum expenditure (both Capital Expenditure and Operating Expenditure) incurred to date, or forecast to be incurred, including a reconciliation of such expenditure against the then applicable Spectrum Plan." This addition to the facility suggested to me that the lender did not believe the company had buyers and wanted to ensure that if the company received a take under, an offer below the stock price, it would be accepted, since it would make the lender whole.

On 10/5/2017, with the 10/31 deadline approaching, GSAT announced a large equity issuance of $125m. What surprised me was that the Chairman could sell 38m shares of stock of stock before 12/31/2017 for 'tax reasons' even though he participated in the equity deal for $20m. I saw this as his taking some money off the table in GSAT.

Meanwhile, the company continued to guide to a second country outside the US where they would receive approval to license or sell their spectrum, potentially unlocking international value to the assets. That second market, however, ended up being Botswana, announced in November 2017. I was surprised management believed that they could unlock value to the stock through an approval in a small, frontier African country.

In December 2017, the Chairman's 38m shares were sold through Morgan Stanley for $1.16/share. Through 2018, with the FCC's announcements of additional spectrum hitting the market and the late 2017 stock issuances, GSAT continued to drift down into the $0.50/share range, where I covered. The company also attempted to merge with another entity controlled by the Chairman, though the merger was challenged by a large GSAT shareholder. This prompted a termination of the merger agreement and an additional equity offering at $0.35/share in December 2018. Two years after FCC approval, the company still has not sold or licensed its spectrum.

TENETS MANIFESTED IN GSAT

Several tenets guided me through the GSAT short. During the idea sourcing phase, I followed the tenet of sticking to what is predictable. My experience in telecom translated to a strong understanding of the industry's direction. In the diligence phase, reading primary sources revealed a significant change in GSAT's plan: its FCC process had not gone well, and its revised proposal seriously limited potential buyers of its spectrum. Following the tenet of empathy, I put myself in the shoes of a carrier like Verizon and concluded that a purchase of GSAT's spectrum would be unlikely, while assessing near-term maturities. Speaking to industry experts and understanding valuation, I realized Wall Street's and the company's view of its spectrum was very different from industry's view, following its failure to get FCC approval for its initial, stronger proposal.

GSAT offers an interesting look at the importance of monitoring regulatory events. Such events, especially in businesses where the company's entire value can hinge on one outcome, can drastically affect business value. Given that the FCC announcement was issued on 12/23/2016 and I began shorting the stock fairly soon after speaks to the importance of doing the right work at the right time and acting quickly when convicted. While I shorted in a very small amount the week of the announcement, the confirmatory datapoints, thereafter, gave me conviction to continue to press the short.

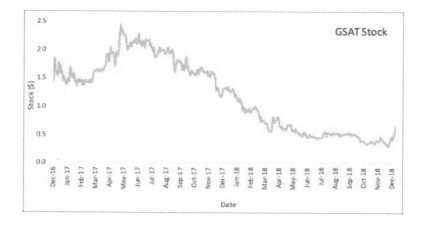

CHAPTER 4: FUSION-IO

SHORTING AN INNOVATOR IN MEMORY AMIDST INCREASING COMPETITION

INTRODUCTION

Fusion-IO (FIO) sold flash-based memory cards that were plugged into the PCIe bus (a connection to plug in a graphics card or hard drive...etc) of a server. Historically, data had been stored on hard drives. However, over the previous several years, data storage had transitioned onto solid state drives (semiconductor-based flash memory) which are faster but much more expensive. These hard drives or solid state drives were located in a storage array, attached to the server. Fusion-IO took this transition one step further by attaching their storage directly into a server via a high bandwidth bus (PCIe) rather than in an attached storage array. The PCIe bus was in the server itself, closer to the brains of the datacenter, so it allowed FIO customers like Facebook to store data customers accessed often (like pictures in a Facebook news feed) more conveniently. As a result, the end-user could access the data more quickly. This innovation allowed FIO to initially maintain sole source supplier status at Apple and Facebook, lending them the credibility to grow their customer base and sell their products at exceptionally high prices and margins.

IDEA SOURCING

I first began following FIO after its IPO in 2011 (IPO Monitoring Tenet) but did not short the stock until mid-2012 after several earnings beats and an acceleration in insider stock sales (Follow Insider Actions Tenet). FIO stood out due to its sole source supplier status at Apple and Facebook (Follow the Actions of the 100LB Gorilla Tenet), and its position as an innovator (Innovators' Dilemma Short Tenet).

DILIGENCE

The initial primary source analysis phase, reading filings/ transcripts and sell-side research, suggested that FIO fit well in the Innovators' Dilemma short category, in which a new, single product company identifies a niche for which they could charge a very high price to large customers with a significant total addressable market because it has the first product of its kind. Post-IPO, management began significantly selling stock (Follow Insider Actions Tenet) through several earnings beats after the IPO. As such, FIO seemed like a juicy short candidate but as previously discussed, the next steps involved identifying and conducting due diligence on competition to determine its price, product quality and timing of deployment. Hence, the next step in my process began, finding industry experts to assess the competitive landscape and total addressable market.

In the next diligence phase, having detailed conversations with experts and reading industry trade journals/whitepapers, I identified three characteristics of FIO that made it an interesting short. First, there was little reason to believe FIO was superior to its competitors. Second, FIO faced a threat from NVMe technology, which would standardize interfaces across SSDs used by the server rather than requiring individual interfaces. Third, FIO faced a threat of disintermediation as NAND manufacturers pursued the enterprise solid state drive space, directly.

FIO's lack of competitive advantage first came to light in a talk with the CTO at a major investment bank. I learned that the bank adopted Virident, an upstart competitor to FIO, so I scheduled a call with the CTO to discuss their decision. He told me that they had been working with FIO for the previous five years and their cards were ahead of their time, solving a bottleneck of accessing data extremely quickly within servers. FIO had iterated the product many times and the latest iteration was great, but the innovation was being replicated at much lower price by new competitors, including Virident. The bank was having a tough time justifying FIO's prices given the competition at much lower prices. At the time, FIO charged $5,000 for a 650GB card vs. Virident at $7,500 for 1.4TB ($7.70/GB for FIO vs. $5.35/GB for Virident). Through further investigations of Virident, I learned they began winning additional

customers, including Kayak and LinkedIn, and getting to
final stages in a number of RFPs against FIO after gaining
the bank as a customer bought them credibility. FIO's lack
of competitive advantage was also reflected by a conversation with Network Appliances, a storage solutions reseller.
Netapp informed me that they wanted a PCIe product on
the market before VMWorld (VMWare's conference) so
they went with FIO but planned on adding new competitors
to their product suite in the near future.

I identified a much bigger issue for FIO, however, while attending the 2012 Flash Summit, an industry conference in
California focused on flash memory and solid state drives.
I pushed myself to attend a number of workshops, despite
my limited knowledge base making the content a bit dry!
After the 5th or 6th seminar, the knowledge began com-
pounding (as it often does) and I hit the holy grail for a FIO
short during a seminar on NVMe. An NVMe based PCIe
card would standardize all interfaces across SSDs used by
the server, requiring only a single driver to work. One can
draw a parallel to consumer flash drives, which plug into a
USB port but do not require individual manufacturer-spe-
cific device software (i.e. I can buy any flash drive from
Amazon, plug it into my USB port and it will work). The
greatest complaint regarding the FIO PCIe card solution, as
described in the seminar, was that it required non-standard,
device-specific software and interfaces which used too much
CPU power. NVMe would standardize PCIe based SSDs
and make them much more efficient, commoditizing hardware providers like FIO in the process. A conversation with

Kaminario, a company that sold SSD arrays, confirmed that NVMe would soon be adopted by everyone in the space. Though the company currently integrated FIO PCIe cards into their array, they planned to shift to competitor products and initially used FIO only because it was the first mover.

The additional major threat against FIO was disintermediation. During a conversation with Smart Modular, a smaller storage provider, I learned that the overall SSD landscape was becoming more commoditized as the NAND manufacturers, themselves, (Micron, Sandisk, Toshiba... etc) looked to create their own enterprise flash products and disintermediate those between them and the end-customers (this is where FIO lies in the supply-chain). To compete with NVMe and other NVMe-based software manufacturers, Smart Modular shared that FIO would have to decouple its software from its hardware. Doing so would significantly reduce their ASPs, margins and earnings power. Furthermore, LSI had a new PCIe SSD that was beginning to take share. A conversation with Sandisk, one such NAND manufacturer, confirmed what I learned from Smart Modular – NAND manufacturers would likely disintermediate companies like FIO. Sandisk had acquired Pliant and Flashsoft to be more competitive in the enterprise solid state drive space, and planned to release a PCIe SSD, similar to FIO's, to the channel level at the end of Q2 2012. EMC and Dell were pushing everyone to move towards a standardized NVMe product.

I spoke with a number of other competitors, customers and suppliers, including Whiptail, Integrated Device

Technology, and Micron. Each conversation lead to the
same conclusion: In the near-term, competition would steal
market share from FIO, causing revenue growth to deceler-
ate. In the medium-term, FIO would have to cut prices to
stay competitive, impairing margins, and in the longer-term,
NVMe would destroy any potential for future growth and
profitability for a single-product PCIe SSD company like
FIO while the NAND manufacturers would sell the hardware, themselves. FIO clearly exhibited multiple tenets past
the sourcing phase, being a higher cost producer of a product customers did not love, facing increasing competition
and low switching costs, and having a significant difference
between the industry and Wall Street view.

VALUATION AND MODELING

While the competitive angle sounded very compelling, the
next step in my process was to see what was actually priced
into the stock since a miss vs. expectations is so important in
short-selling. Understanding expectations can mean the difference between losing and making money in a short even as
the fundamental case plays out in both scenarios. For example, revenues may decline for a community newspaper, while
I estimated FIO revenues may still growth 8-10%. FIO,
however, is priced for perfection at 50-60x forward EPS and
30-40% revenue growth, numbers that can be disproved
based on my research, while a community newspaper stock
is priced for bankruptcy in several years at 3-4x EPS, hence
the revenue declines are already expected. Should the tail on
the newspaper last longer than very low expectations (even if

revenue remains flat), the stock could rise significantly while
FIO was already priced to continue growing revenue at 30-
40% and maintain 100% market share in the PCIe SSD space.
As discussed in the innovators' dilemma short tenet, I can win
in multiple ways on FIO with a significant margin of safety.

Putting the analysis together, I arrived at a variant to consensus opinion on FIO based on the following analysis.

FIO faced increasing competition. LSI was launching their
Nytro product (competitive to FIO) in Q2/Q3 2012 with
availability through Oracle in Q3 and Cisco/IBM in Q4.
They had revenue in the 'double digit' millions at the time
and expected they would grow faster than the market. They
thought market growth was 40%/year. They also had just
won a large contract at a social network (either Facebook or
LinkedIn). Virident had won a bulge bracket bank, as discussed above, and Virident was being very price aggressive
at a 30-40% discount to FIO's pricing to steal share. Micron
had launched a single layer NAND PCIe card (higher cost)
at the same price as FIO but was qualifying an MLC card
(lower cost NAND) at a price discount to FIO. IDT was in the
process of bringing NVMe based products onto the market.

Given the increased price competition, I expected FIO
ASPs to drop 5% in their core revenue (all customers excluding Facebook/Apple) in the December 2012 quarter, with
declines increasing to 12-17% over the following years and
strategic revenue ASPs declining faster.

	Sep-11	Dec-11	Mar-12	Jun-12	FY2012	Sep-12	Dec-12	Mar-13	Jun-13	FY2013	Sep-13	Dec-13	Mar-14	Jun-14	FY2014
Revenue	74,385	84,131	94,237	106,596	359,349	118,115	117,729	122,527	133,781	492,151	140,009	139,547	145,216	158,442	583,214
Growth	175%	169%	40%	49%	82%	59%	40%	30%	26%	37%	19%	19%	19%	18%	19%
Units	10,306	11,900	13,745	15,533	51,485	17,173	17,850	20,352	22,996	78,371	24,594	25,543	29,127	32,903	112,166
Growth	159%	192%	42%	53%		67%	50%	48%	48%	52%	43%	43%	43%	43%	43%
ASPs	7,217	7,070	6,856	6,862	6,980	6,878	6,596	6,020	5,818	6,280	5,693	5,463	4,986	4,815	5,200
Growth	6%	-8%	5%	-3%		-5%	-7%	-12%	-15%	-10%	-17%	-17%	-17%	-17%	-17%
Core Revenue	33,473	36,176	42,407	50,100	162,156	51,616	51,551	54,111	61,748	219,027	59,978	59,903	62,877	71,752	254,509
Growth	263%	43%	186%	100%	118%	54%	43%	28%	23%	35%	16%	16%	16%	16%	16%
Units	4,062	4,522	5,301	6,086	19,971	6,141	6,783	7,686	8,825	29,435	8,598	9,496	10,761	12,355	41,209
Growth	252%	43%	186%	104%		51%	50%	45%	45%	47%	40%	40%	40%	40%	40%
ASPs	8,240	8,000	8,000	8,232	8,120	8,405	7,600	7,040	6,997	7,441	6,976	6,308	5,843	5,808	6,176
Growth	3%	0%	0%	-2%		2%	-5%	-12%	-15%	-8%	-17%	-17%	-17%	-17%	-17%
Strategic Revenue	40,912	47,955	51,830	56,496	197,193	66,499	66,177	68,416	72,032	273,124	80,031	79,645	82,339	86,691	328,705
Growth	130%	701%	7%	21%	66%	63%	38%	32%	28%	39%	20%	20%	20%	20%	20%
Units	6,244	7,378	8,444	9,447	31,513	11,032	11,066	12,666	14,171	48,936	15,996	16,046	18,366	20,548	70,957
Growth	252%	43%	186%	104%		77%	50%	50%	50%	55%	45%	45%	45%	45%	45%
ASPs	6,552	6,500	6,138	5,980	6,257	6,028	5,980	5,401	5,083	5,581	5,003	4,963	4,483	4,219	4,632
Growth	3%	0%	0%	-2%		-8%	-8%	-12%	-15%	-11%	-17%	-17%	-17%	-17%	-17%

However, I still expected some volume growth because the overall market was growing very quickly.

	Sep-11	Dec-11	Mar-12	Jun-12	FY2012	Sep-12	Dec-12	Mar-13	Jun-13	FY2013	Sep-13	Dec-13	Mar-14	Jun-14	FY2014
COS	27,354	41,206	45,180	45,305	159,045	47,994	50,882	56,276	61,678	216,830	64,645	65,124	72,035	78,932	280,736
COS/Unit	2,654	3,463	3,287	2,917	3,089	2,795	2,851	2,765	2,682	2,767	2,628	2,550	2,473	2,399	2,503
Seq Change			30%	-5%	-11%	-4%	2%	-3%	-3%	-10%	-2%	-3%	-3%	-3%	-10%
Gross Profit	47,031	42,925	49,057	61,291	200,304	70,121	66,847	66,251	72,103	275,321	75,364	74,423	73,181	79,510	502,478
Gross Margin	63.2%	51.0%	52.1%	57.5%	55.7%	59.4%	56.8%	54.1%	53.9%	55.9%	53.8%	53.3%	50.4%	50.2%	51.9%
S&M	17,477	20,265	23,012	26,417	87,171	25,020	27,272	29,726	32,402	114,420	32,402	32,402	32,402	32,402	129,607
% of Revenue	23.5%	24.1%	24.4%	24.8%	24.3%	21.2%	23.2%	24.3%	24.2%	23.2%	23.1%	23.2%	22.3%	20.5%	22.2%
R&D	10,787	12,823	15,263	18,797	57,670	20,912	22,794	24,846	27,082	95,633	27,082	27,082	27,082	27,082	108,327
% of Revenue	14.5%	15.2%	16.2%	17.6%	16.0%	17.7%	18.4%	20.3%	20.3%	19.4%	19.3%	19.4%	18.6%	17.1%	18.6%
G&A	12,417	13,222	15,050	16,408	57,097	15,084	16,442	17,921	18,534	68,981	19,534	19,534	19,534	19,534	78,137
% of Revenue	16.7%	15.7%	16.0%	15.4%	15.9%	12.8%	14.0%	14.6%	14.6%	14.0%	14.0%	14.0%	13.3%	12.3%	13.4%
EBIT	6,350	-3,385	-4,268	-331	-1,634	9,105	340	6,242	-6,915	-3,713	3,653	-4,595	-5,836	493	-13,592
Margin	8.5%	-4.0%	-4.5%	-0.3%	-0.5%	7.7%	0.3%	-5.1%	-5.2%	-0.8%	-2.6%	-3.3%	-4.0%	0.3%	-2.3%
Non-GAAP EBIT	16,126	6,572	7,199	11,907	41,804	22,994	13,725	7,246	6,923	50,988	11,901	9,523	8,281	14,639	64,344
Margin	21.7%	7.8%	7.6%	11.2%	11.6%	19.5%	11.7%	5.9%	5.2%	10.3%	8.5%	6.8%	5.7%	9.2%	7.6%
Interest Income	37	50	81	90	258	55	96	95	95	341	126	129	132	136	521
PBT	6,387	-3,335	-4,187	-241	-1,376	9,160	435	-6,147	-6,820	-3,372	-3,528	-4,466	-5,705	628	-13,070
Margin	8.6%	-4.0%	-4.4%	-0.2%	-0.4%	7.8%	0.4%	-5.0%	-5.1%	-0.7%	-2.5%	-3.2%	-3.9%	0.4%	-2.2%
Taxes	-1,726	1,021	-167	1,487	615	4,571	152	0	0	4,723	0	0	0	220	220
Rate	-27.0%	-30.6%	4.0%	-617.0%	-44.7%	49.9%	35.0%	35.0%	35.0%	-140.1%	35.0%	35.0%	35.0%	35.0%	-1.7%
ESOP	9,776	9,957	11,467	12,238	43,438	13,889	13,385	13,488	13,838	54,600	15,554	14,118	14,117	14,146	57,936
Non-GAAP Net Income	17,889	5,601	7,447	10,510	41,447	18,478	13,668	7,341	7,018	46,505	12,027	9,652	8,413	14,555	44,646
Margin	24.0%	6.7%	7.9%	9.9%	11.5%	15.6%	11.6%	6.0%	5.2%	9.4%	8.6%	6.9%	5.8%	9.2%	7.7%
FD S/O	108,454	105,744	108,466	107,614		108,425	112,172	115,976	118,619	112,133	121,251	123,746	126,165	128,496	125,011
EPS	0.17	0.05	0.07	0.10	0.39	0.17	0.12	0.06	0.06	0.41	0.10	0.08	0.07	0.11	0.36

Based on the declining revenue and margins, I expected FIO to miss street estimates in FY2014 by a wide margin, in which case the stock would trade down from the high $20s to the high single digits at 20x FY14 EPS of $0.36.

TAM Analysis – imputing the numbers above into a total addressable market/market share analysis allowed me to gut check my assumptions on market share changes for FIO.

	Sep-11	Dec-11	Mar-12	Jun-12	FY2012	Sep-12	Dec-12	Mar-13	Jun-13	FY2013	Sep-13	Dec-13	Mar-14	Jun-14	FY2014
Market Size	74,385	84,131	94,237	106,596	359,349	131,239	135,176	148,694	169,511	584,619	203,413	213,584	224,263	257,902	899,161
Market Growth						76.4%	60.7%	57.8%	59.0%	62.7%	55.0%	58.0%	50.8%	52.1%	53.8%
FIO Market Share	100.0%	100.0%	100.0%	100.0%	100.0%	90.0%	87.1%	82.4%	78.9%	84.2%	68.8%	65.3%	64.8%	61.4%	64.9%
Competitors	0	0	0	0		2	3	4	6		8	10	12	12	
Market Share Each						5.0%	4.3%	4.4%	3.5%		3.9%	3.5%	2.9%	3.2%	
Aggregate Market Share						10.0%	12.9%	17.6%	21.1%		31.2%	34.7%	35.2%	38.6%	

I assumed, based on my conversations, that FIO had a 90% market share in Q3 2012, declining as more competitors entered the market. LSI has said they have 'double digit millions' in revenue from their PCIe product in just a single quarter, as discussed above. They expected the market to grow at 40%/year for the foreseeable future, lower than some sell-side estimates of a $2bln market by the end of 2014 (80% implied growth). I believe the problem with the sell-side estimates of the TAM was that they were not taking into account ASP declines from competition—they were assuming that gross margins would stay intact and everyone in the market priced where FIO was at the time, which was impossible given how much higher PCIe gross margins were vs. every other storage product out there. I also concluded that as LSI and other competitors took share, even if I assumed the market was growing at 60+% in FY13 and 54% in 2014, to get to my revenue assumptions, FIO would still have 60+% market share in a $900mln market, which is not aggressive at all. This implies that there are 12 major competitors by the end of FY14 and each has only a 3% market share.

FRAMING THE BULL CASE

A bulge bracket investment bank initiated coverage of FIO in late 2012 with a $32 price target based on 50x $0.63 in EPS. The report highlighted FIO's first mover advantage in

PCIe flash and key relationships with Apple, Facebook and Salesforce.com. They also emphasized that FIO had potential to add software to their products, which would increase gross margins and OEM relationships with HP, Cisco, Dell and EMC. Clearly, my research told me many of these supposed strengths were actually weaknesses.

SETUP AND CONCLUSION

FIO was a very juicy short, priced for perfection in an industry where the sell-side analysts were not properly vetting the changing competitive environment and extrapolated high initial growth too far into the future, so I shorted it in Q2/Q3 2012. Extremely detailed diligence through industry trade shows and conversations with competitors, customers, and suppliers yielded consistent evidence that pricing was declining and NVMe would blow up FIO's entire business model, making it a phenomenal short with 60-75% downside over the following two years.

CQ4 Earnings – when the company reported CQ4 earnings on 1/31/2013, the stock dropped 13% to $17 (well below where I shorted in the high $20s as the market began to see competition, even before the earnings announcement). The company blamed their earnings miss on a delay in product shipments and while I was excited by the initial drop, my diligence made me confident that this was only the beginning. I increased the size of my short because I believed competition was increasing. Competitors EMC, IDTI and STX were all discussing their foray into PCIe

SSD cards in their earnings calls, validating my thesis of increased competition.

CQ1 Earnings – the company reported another earnings miss and guided down their fiscal year on 5/8/13 with the stock dropping another 19% to $14. Competition was taking share and I saw it manifested in the numbers. As I continued to monitor the original investment thesis to ensure it didn't change, I uncovered additional facts to support the nearing obsolescence of FIO. The throughput between SSD arrays (outside of the server) and the server was improving, which meant data stored on an array could be called up almost as quickly as data stored on a PCIe card. Confirming this new datapoint, all venture capital money in the space (which tends to favor where spaces move) was invested in new array companies, and not in a single new PCIe SSD company like FIO.

I covered the short in the $9-10 range in December 2013 as the thesis had played out.

TENETS MANIFESTED IN FIO

Several tenets guided me through the Fusion-IO short. During the idea sourcing phase, following 100LB gorillas like Apple and Facebook, both of which were customers of Fusion-IO, and following IPOs, the point in time that I began tracking Fusion-IO, proved integral. Fusion-IO stood out in this phase due to its potential to be an innovator's dilemma situation. It was a first mover, but as I found out while speaking to experts during the diligence phase, it was being disintermediated and left behind by new NVMe technology (with low switching costs). During the diligence phase, I also read primary sources, which exposed insider selling and confirmed my suspicion that the increased competition (from vendors with a lower cost structure/lower point on the cost curve) would bring FIO down. After so much diligence, FIO felt right – a predictable change in technology from multiple directions where Wall Street metrics (revenue and gross margins) began breaking down.

The case of FIO offers a very good look at what one can uncover by doing copious amounts of diligence and speaking to industry participants across the supply chain. It's not always easy. It takes time to read, learn and understand such a complex business, and it takes scrappiness to get in front of the right people to ask the right questions. If done properly and if the stock is shorted right as sentiment is highest but the industry view inflects down, we can time a short and do pretty well!

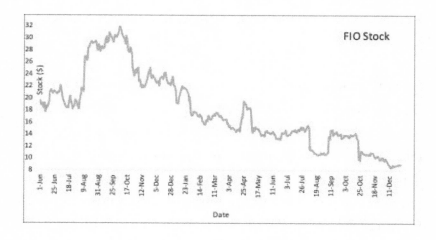

CHAPTER 5:

UNITED NATURAL FOODS

SHORTING A DISTRIBUTOR DISINTERMEDIATED

BY ITS LARGEST CUSTOMER AFTER A CHANGE

OF CONTROL

INTRODUCTION

United Natural Foods (UNFI) distributes organic and natural foods, most of which are dry or shelf-stable, to grocery
stores around the US. Whole Foods, a large independent or-
ganic/natural grocery store chain, accounted for about 1/3
of UNFI's revenue as of early 2018. The company's contract
with Whole Foods was to run through 2025. Aside from
their business with Whole Foods, UNFI distributed food to
independent natural grocers (another 1/3 of revenue) and
large, conventional supermarket chains (last 1/3 of revenue).
The company owned 33 Distribution Centers, representing
~8.7 million square feet of warehouse space, carrying over
110,000 SKUs from more than 9,000 suppliers and serv-
ing over 43,000 customer locations, hence very well scaled.
As healthy, natural and white label food has become more

popular over the last couple decades, UNFI's business has
grown significantly. While many grocers source higher turn-
ing inventory and foods from the major consumer packaging
companies directly, lower turn, niche natural foods tend
to be distributed through independent groups like UNFI.
Given the large mix of such foods at Whole Foods, utilizing
UNFI's distribution channel was a natural fit, pun intended. UNFI cited as its competitive advantage the 33 distribution centers that position them closer to their customers
than their regional, independent competitors, and provide
them with lower inbound freight costs. UNFI also points to
its customer relationships (trust built over years from fulfill-
ment of orders, timely product of delivery, competitive prices,
high level of product marketing support) and claims natural
distributors compete on distribution service levels, depth of
inventory selection, price and quality of customer service.

IDEA SOURCING

In mid-2017, Amazon announced the acquisition of Whole
Foods and, in my regular course of monitoring the actions of
the 100LB gorilla (a sourcing tenet), I assessed how I could
potentially play this structural change in the grocery industry, long or short. As such, in assessing Porter's Five Forces
for Whole Foods (WFM), I saw that a significant portion
of their cost of goods sold line (i.e. supplier relationships)
was concentrated with UNFI so I began to evaluate how
Amazon might shift away from outside distributors, especially given their own vast distribution center and transpor-
tation logistics network, the lowest cost in just about any

industry. Meanwhile, UNFI management continued to sell significant amounts of stock in late 2017/early 2018 (Follow Insider Actions Tenet).

DILIGENCE

I began my analysis by reading through the publicly available (though significantly redacted) contract between WFM and UNFI to assess whether WFM had any ability to re-negotiate the contract, especially in a change of control. I also began my practical diligence by speaking to grocery supply chain experts and past Amazon logistics employees to develop a better understanding of Amazon's longer-term strategy with WFM. My diligence process lead me to two scenarios in which a short in UNFI could work. In the first case, AMZN shifts sourcing away from UNFI into their own AMZN distribution beast. In the second case, AMZN increases WFM distribution through UNFI, 'crowding out' higher-margin UNFI sales to independent natural grocery chains.

AMZN Taking Distribution In-House – According to former Amazon employees and supply chain/logistics experts in the space, Amazon would likely shift over the following three years to create combined distribution centers for Prime Pantry, Amazon Fresh and Whole Foods. Doing so would increase/combine purchasing power of these entities, especially in the top 40 metro markets, allowing AMZN to target half of the US population. Industry experts also confirmed that the contract between AMZN and UNFI was set up to allow an 'out' if either company wanted it. WFM

would be able to end the contract, and UNFI then had the
option to try and re-negotiate lower contract pricing in order to retain WFM/AMZN. I also learned from industry
experts that over time, they expected Amazon to shift WFM
away from a natural/organic grocery store chain towards a
mass market chain (for example, soon after the acquisition,
they began selling Vitamin Water at WFM) which would
disfavor the goods UNFI distributed to WFM.

UNFI Distributes to WFM at Lower Prices – Many industry
experts believed that while AMZN might shift WFM opera-
tions away from UNFI, sales were probably safe in the near
term. However, I spoke to a few who corroborated my belief
that UNFI sold to WFM at a lower price/gross margin than
its other independent customers since WFM was such a large
customer (purchasing power). This proved beneficial to the
short thesis since I believed a crowding-out effect might occur given the increased volumes and pricing promotions I
started to see Amazon push through WFM. Put simply, if
UNFI was on the hook for increased distribution due to lower prices at WFM, it would crowd out their higher margin
distribution and thereby impair earnings power in the short-
run while Amazon disintermediated them in the long run.

FRAMING THE BULL CASE

The sell-side was less sanguine on UNFI than some of the
other shorts discussed in the book but even still, an investment bank initiated coverage on the company in mid-2017
with a neutral rating and a $40 price target. The perspective

was based on UNFI's leading position in the organic food space, but also acknowledged struggles with Whole Foods and uncertainty around Amazon's strategic direction. That said, a neutral rating is far from a sell rating based on the short thesis!

SETUP AND CONCLUSION

Based on a likely near-term earnings impairment and a long-term term replacement, I shorted UNFI in early 2018.

UNFI slightly beat earnings estimates through early/mid 2018 as volumes increased through WFM with AMZN's price promotions, but margins started to decline beginning in their FQ3 2018 (4/30/18 quarter). Despite 11.8% yoy revenue growth (mainly due to WFM), the company made an accounting change that might have masked a decline in gross margins as I saw the short thesis beginning to play out.

In July 2018, UNFI announced their intention to buy Supervalu (SVU) a grocery store chain and divest SVU's grocery store chain, then integrate SVU's distribution business with UNFI. I viewed the deal as a way to diversify revenue away from a likely declining revenue/margin exposure to WFM.

In September 2018, UNFI reported adjusted EPS of $0.76 vs. FactSet consensus at $0.86 and FY19 guidance of $3.48-3.58 in EPS vs. FactSet at $3.54 and commentary that the bottom-line in the quarter was impacted by a customer mix shift at lower gross margins.

In December 2018, UNFI reported FQ1 EPS of $0.59 which missed FactSet consensus of $0.73, despite revenue of $2.87bln vs. FactSet consensus of $2.70bln. Management blamed the miss on SVU's business and maintained that their core UNFI business held up in the quarter. While we do not know what exactly happened with UNFI's core business with WFM because SVU's somewhat obfuscated earnings, I believe that my thesis was likely sound and UNFI's stock price declined, accordingly.

TENETS MANIFESTED IN UNFI

I sourced the UNFI short idea by watching the 100LB Gorilla, which in this case was AMZN. I assessed Porter's Five Forces and found the situation favorable for shorting UNFI, and an uptick in insider action further validated my suspicions. The primary source, in this case a contract between AMZN and UNFI, and discussions with industry experts during the diligence phase confirmed that in any scenario, AMZN's acquisition of WFM would likely cause UNFI's revenue to decline, prompting me to short the stock.

I included this chapter in the book to illustrate that shorting does not have to involve understanding an extremely esoteric tech product to gain an edge. Simply following Porter's Five Forces in situations where large changes happen to a big customer allows us to identify the right ponds in which to fish. Then, it's simply a matter of reading everything we can and finding the right people with whom to talk and ask the right questions. The time spent on a UNFI short was much shorter than any of the other shorts in this book, but it yielded a great result, too!

CHAPTER 6:

IMAGINATION TECHNOLOGIES

SHORTING AN INTELLECTUAL PROPERTY
BUSINESS AHEAD OF A CHANGE BY ITS
LARGEST CUSTOMER

INTRODUCTION

Imagination Technologies (IMG LN) is a provider of intellectual property (IP) for graphics processors (73% of their revenue) and internet-of-things architectures. IMG provides its IP to phone and semiconductor manufacturers of graphics processor units (GPUs) that use its instruction set (or design code/architecture) in exchange for a royalty stream of revenues. At the time that I began researching IMG in late 2016, Apple was IMG's largest customer, accounting for an estimated 60% of IMG's revenue and likely all of its operating income in GPU royalties, an extremely high margin business.

IDEA SOURCING

In September of 2016, I received a phone call from an industry expert and friend, David Kanter, who had just attended the 2016 Apple Worldwide Developers' Conference. He sat in on a seminar by Apple engineers entitled "Advanced Metal Shader Optimization" which highlighted detailed tuning guidelines and architectural details for a custom GPU. The details for the custom GPU were very different from those of Apple's current GPU, the IMG PowerVR Series 6 GPU. This led him to believe that Apple was shifting from licensing IMG's PowerVR GPUs towards developing and designing an internal, custom, proprietary GPU. With this shift, Apple would cease making royalty payments to IMG. Apple's CPU (the chip that is the brains of the iPhone) is a precedent for such a switch. On early iPhones, Apple used a CPU licensed by Arm Technologies, to which it paid royalties, much like IMG. This CPU was later swapped out for a custom version on later iPhones, suggesting the same may happen for the GPU. Such a shift would be catastrophic for IMG's revenue and earnings power. From here, I went on to better understanding the architecture of the GPU, proving the thesis and assessing timing.

DILIGENCE

This case made use of an unconventional primary source: open job listings, which provided evidence of a shift to proprietary graphics. I combed through Apple's open positions to conclude that since 2009, Apple had been hiring graphics architects and driver developers from industry leaders such as AMD, Intel, Google, and Nvidia (based on LinkedIn profiles). At the time, Apple had posted more than 50 open positions for graphics engineers working on hardware and software design, clearly showing that they were building design teams for their own GPU.

An additional primary source would become important later: the terms of the contract between Apple and IMG, which I could glean from both companies' press releases. Reading the press releases informed me that the contract had last been extended in February 2014 for a multi-year period.

In order for app developers to adjust to Apple's new GPU, they would need to know how to write programs suited for it. The main change regarded the Shader Core, the part of the GPU that executes shading, color, and pixelation. Apple engineers explained how app developers would have to adapt to it in the "Advanced Metal Shader Optimization" presentation at WWDC 2016, described to me earlier by David after he attended the conference. Apple engineers provided detailed instructions for amending old apps and writing new ones for a proprietary Apple GPU vs. the Imagination GPU. Comparing the available details for the two GPUs made the distinctions clear. In particular, (1) Apple used a different register file than IMG and (2) its data conversion functions looked like they were more efficient in power and performance than IMG's.

1. Register File – The two major formats of register files
    are 16-bit half precision and 32-bit single precision
    calculations. While 16-bit is generally less accurate, it
    is sufficient for graphics because most displays range
    from 8-12 bits per pixel. Apple's engineers emphasized
    that using 16-bit offers twice the performance and
    twice the power efficiency of 32-bit, making it clear that
    their architecture is focused on 16-bit primary design
    point. In contrast, the IMG PowerVR Series 6 and 7
    GPUs use 32-bit registers. The distinction provides
    further evidence that Apple is moving away from
    Imagination's GPU design.

2. Data Conversion Function – While 16-bit has the
    advantages described above, it's often not precise enough
    for large blocks of color. From Apple's presentations
    to developers, I learned they offered developers the
    advantage of seamless conversion between 16-bit
    and 32-bit at the hardware level. On the other hand,
    Imagination's PowerVR's optimization manual states
    that data conversion has a cost (not as seamless as what
    Apple communicated) and recommends that developers
    write programs to minimize the number of conversions.
    This clearly means Apple is using its own data conversion
    functions, which are superior to Imagination's.

Clearly, Apple was developing an internal GPU. Apple had
an obvious strategic rationale for doing so – greater platform control and differentiation. The same strategy likely
motivated Apple's earlier switch to an internal CPU. In

early CPU designs, Apple used standard ARM CPU cores designed and manufactured by Samsung. Starting with the iPhone 5, Apple switched to a custom, internally-designed CPU that now offers best-in-class performance, eclipsing ARM, Qualcomm, and Samsung.

I concluded that a custom GPU provided four strategic advantages for Apple:

1. Superior performance and power efficiency: Apple's iPhone 6S had the best performance on almost every smartphone benchmark and unlike the competition, didn't suffer any overheating problems. The iPhone 7 was 40-50% faster for graphics, clearly differentiating the product. Apple's developer tools took advantage of the GPU for image processing and machine learning applications and were accessible to third party developers. Instagram, for example, could use Apple's tools to improve the filters on pictures.

2. Capability to develop new features and fix bugs in their custom GPU without helping competitors: Imitation is a sincere form of flattery and with a standard licensed GPU from Imagination, changes Apple makes are available to Samsung, Mediatek and all of Imagination's other customers. Apple's proprietary design is harder to copy and preserves differentiation for the company.

3. Improved time-to-market and lowered schedule risk: With an in-house design, Apple could invest in engineering as much as necessary to hit product release dates and

maximize quality control. In contrast, Imagination simply had fewer resources available.

4. Reduced dependence on suppliers: Apple avoids single-source components and always encourages alternate providers (e.g., choosing Intel's LTE modem for iPhone 7 as an alternative to Qualcomm). Apple had already built a large GPU design and software team, which can develop fixed-function graphics hardware if necessary. An internally designed GPU is a highly effective second-source which gives the company excellent leverage in negotiations.

The remaining question, however, was why Apple would still pay IMG in 2016 if the switch happened beginning with the iPhone 6 in 2014.

VALUATION AND MODELING

While I did not know the specific terms of Apple's agreement with Imagination, I returned to the primary sources, Apple and Imagination press releases. The press releases revealed that their agreement was extended for a multi-year period in February 2014, before the launch of the iPhone 6. However, it was apparent based on the aforementioned points that IMG was providing less value to Apple in 2016 vs. pre-2014. Apple was continuing to expand their internal team and make their own GPU better with each iteration, and IMG was losing leverage with Apple.

SETUP AND CONCLUSION

Given that this was a multi-year agreement that began in February 2014, I concluded that by 2017/2018, the renewal economics (if any) should be significantly lower, so I shorted the stock in October 2016 at about 250p. On April 3, 2017, shares dropped to 103p when Imagination announced that its largest customer, Apple would stop using its products in 15-24 months since Apple was developing its own internal graphics processing unit, reducing its reliance on IMG's technology.

TENETS MANIFESTED IN IMG

Sourcing the idea for IMG came from maintaining a rolo-dex of experts/friends watching the 100LB gorilla – Apple. In the diligence phase, my process involved a creative use of primary sources, including job postings and press releases. I made use of information gleaned from the conversation that sparked the idea, and eventually predicted when the stock would drop.

I included IMG in this book because it further shows the value of staying in front of industry contacts, doing very de-tailed diligence on a small European company where most investors and sell-side analysts are 'asleep at the wheel' despite the business risks that come from such high customer concen-tration. In such a situation, it takes only one small move by a customer to drastically affect the outcomes of its supplier.

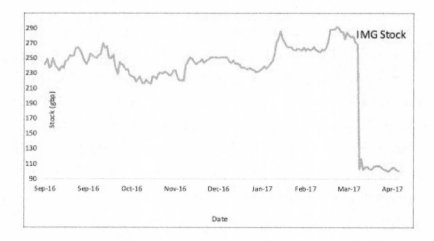

CHAPTER 7: ELPIDA

SHORTING A HIGH COST PRODUCER WITH BALANCE SHEET RISK AMIDST LOWER DEMAND

INTRODUCTION

Elpida manufactures dynamic random access memory (DRAM) semiconductor chips used in devices like computers, servers, mobile phones, and tablets. DRAM is used within the processor to access short bursts of memory required to run programs. Unlike hard disk drive or flash memory, DRAM does not store data. Increasing DRAM increases the number of programs that can run at once, and thus the speed of the computer. Elpida was one of seven major DRAM manufacturers in the world when I began studying the business in 2011.

IDEA SOURCING

In the Autumn of 2011, I read an interesting report about Samsung's lead in DRAM and NAND memory. That lead allowed them to produce at a lower cost than competitors. At the same time, industry reports on DRAM and NAND discussed potential secular declines in DRAM demand based on new, more efficient computer and mobile phone software. The potential to find a loser in an industry with a significantly varied cost structure and potentially slowing demand piqued my interest. I assessed all the players, discussed with a future colleague, and Elpida seemed to be in a weak position with a large amount of debt coming due in early 2012 (Industry Cost Curve and Near-Term Maturity Tenets). As such, I began delving deeper into the industry cost structure and longer-term supply and demand.

DILIGENCE

I began my work by reading through Elpida's filings, transcripts and sell-side research, along with those of competitors, Samsung, Hynix, Micron, Nanya, Promos and Powerchip. My intent was to better understand the overall industry structure and assess each company's perspective on future industry supply and demand. I supplemented primary and secondary sources with industry experts across DRAM, most notably an independent consultant formerly an executive at memory company, Smart Modular.

The big picture conclusion from my industry conversations and in-depth reading was that the DRAM industry had the same commodity-like characteristics of most semiconductor industries, driven by Moore's Law. Moore's Law dictates a yearly increasing of power paired with lower costs. The trend results in increased manufacturing supply as industry participants invest capex dollars to supply more chips per given wafer (a wafer is the raw material used to produce a chip) and reduce costs. Let's say Company A and B each produces 100 semiconductor chips per semiconductor wafer at node X (a node is the level of manufacturing advancement at which a chip is produced – a newer/lower node means better/ more chips produced using newer technology). If Company A spends the capex dollars to move to the newer node Y (that is, they invest in manufacturing equipment that allows the laser to refract with twice the size precision), they can now get 200 chips per wafer at node Y without adding more manufacturing lines because the new equipment can etch and cut more precisely, hence smaller chips. Now, Company A is operating at a point in the cost curve about 50% lower than Company B (since they get double the chips per wafer), so Company B must either follow suit and spend the capex dollars or risk losing out on margins and fare worse on the industry cost curve. This also means that Company A's quantity supplied doubles since they now get 200 chips out of a wafer. This case highlights the importance of the industry cost curve tenet in our short criteria.

My research on DRAM showed that companies generated enough cash in the good times to spend capex dollars and move to the newer node. In the bad times, however, they flooded the market in a competitive race to the bottom due to the high fixed cost nature of the business. Thus, they failed to generate enough cash flow in a downturn to spend the capex dollars to keep reducing their cost by getting to the next new node. Samsung, the industry leader, however, continued to spend through the ups and downs of the cycle (given the cash flow it generates from so many other businesses) to ensure its position as the lowest cost producer on the industry cost curve since they continued to move to the newer node and over time, manufactured on nodes 3-4x more advanced than competitors. While each of Samsung's competitors had been able to limp along as demand outstripped supply, they would struggle to do so with demand inflecting downwards, as discussed above. Plateauing DRAM demand leaves higher cost producers like Elpida unable to compete.

Prior to that point, demand grew enough that industry players simply held manufacturing capacity (supply) constant in times of lower demand (where bit growth from moving to the newer node sufficed) and increased capacity in higher demand environments. Since I estimated demand would start secularly plateauing, I believed ASPs would also begin declining since supply automatically increased due to newer nodes yielding a greater number of chips per wafer. As such, the industry supply was essentially stuck at 30-50% bit growth (amount of chips/memory produced) even without increases in capacity. Since demand could not keep up with such innate supply growth going forward, ASPs would fall.

At this point, the next step in my analysis of Elpida's pricing and earnings power was understanding industry supply and demand. To analyze supply, I built an industry cost curve by determining each industry participant's different manufacturing nodes. To determine overall demand, I looked at each market segment that used DRAM (i.e. computers, servers...etc) and estimated content per box (the amount of DRAM per computer or phone...etc) and quantity of boxes (end market product volume). The price point at which demand met supply would determine overall DRAM prices. I could then use the overall price to determine how much Elpida would supply at that price and the amount of revenue and earnings it would garner based on its ASPs and volumes.

Starting with supply, it was common knowledge once I learned the industry through my reading and conversations that different nodes produced a fixed number of chips or Gigabits (Gbs) from a single wafer. The price per wafer was also a known quantity. See the chart below for price per wafer and different amounts of bits (or chips) produced at each node (expressed in nanometers, nm).

Wafer Costs & Chips/Wafer	
Wafer Cost	$1,220
Package/Test Cost per Chip	$0.50
Chips/Wafer	
56nm (1 GB)	1,300
46nm (2 GB)	1,100
32nm (2 GB)	1,800
26nm(2 GB)	2,200
66nm(1 GB)	863
54nm(1 GB)	1,355
44nm(1 GB)	2,100
38nm(1 GB)	3,570
28nm(1 GB)	5,534
90nm(1 GB)	450
50nm(1 GB)	1,450
42nm(1 GB)	2,200
32nm(1 GB)	3,700

Based on my industry conversations, I also determined the yields at different manufacturing levels. Yield describes the percentage of chips per wafer that were usable as opposed to defective. For example, if Samsung had an 85% yield on a particular node that produced 100 chips per wafer, they could use 85 and the other 15 would be defective. Yields varied based on newness of the node because more experience with a manufacturing node reduced error rate.

From here, I determined the cost per Gb for a particular node. I estimated a wafer to cost $1,220 as per the chart above plus $0.50 in packaging/testing costs. At the 56nm process, I estimated 1,300 1Gb chips/wafer were produced with an 85% yield. Dividing total costs by total chips, the cost to produce a 1Gb chip at that node would be $1.60 or ($1,220/(1,300*85%))+$0.50.

I took this information and applied it to all four manufacturing nodes at Samsung, all five at Hynix, all four at Micron and all six at Elpida with the corresponding yields and total production at each company. Blending each of these costs per Gb results in the cost per manufacturer and the overall industry cost curve. Not a simple feat!

	2009	2010	1Q11	2Q11	3Q11	4Q11	2011	1Q12	2Q12	3Q12	4Q12	2012	1Q13	2Q13	3Q13	4Q13	2013
Samsung Production	3,252	5,474	1,936	2,002	2,129	2,342	8,409	2,565	2,670	2,800	2,873	11,008	3,501	3,723	3,995	4,301	15,519
Blended Cost		1.18	1.04	0.98	0.93	0.87	0.95	0.84	0.80	0.75	0.74	0.79	0.65	0.63	0.60	0.58	0.61
ASP		2.76	1.72	1.72	1.41												
Hynix Production	2,431	3,366	1,055	1,142	1,221	1,451	4,868	1,557	1,609	1,784	1,880	6,880	2,018	2,227	2,545	2,757	9,547
Blended Cost		1.51	1.55	1.55	1.43	1.29	1.46	1.25	1.20	1.13	1.10	1.17	1.05	1.00	0.98	0.90	0.97
ASP		2.40	1.66	1.63	1.16												
Micron Production	1,139	1,602	618	628	673	660	2,578	709	714	825	1,013	3,261	1,160	1,258	1,317	1,876	5,111
Blended Cost		1.28	1.58	1.57	1.50	1.46	1.53	1.37	1.35	1.23	1.11	1.26	1.02	0.99	0.96	0.93	0.97
ASP		3.02	2.01	1.84	1.35												
Elpida Production	2,100	2,805	800	1,020	1,067	1,059	3,956	1,160	1,329	1,382	1,488	5,359	1,530	1,605	1,687	1,783	6,605
Blended Cost		1.76	1.29	1.38	1.10	1.05	1.20	0.94	0.83	0.81	0.77	0.84	0.73	0.70	0.68	0.66	0.69
ASP		2.43	1.43	1.31	0.81												

While this analysis sounds simplistic in hindsight, working to determine all these numbers for each industry participant took many, many hours of reading and industry conversations. This data is, of course, somewhat inaccurate in hindsight but based on the information available, I used it to determine Elpida's earnings power.

PREDICTING INDUSTRY DEMAND

I predicted industry demand by assessing the PC/Notebook, Server, Tablet/Ultrabook, and Phone segment as follows.

PC/Notebook Demand for Commodity DRAM – Most industry groups predicted at the time that PC/Notebook sales should increase at mid-high single digits in 2012 and 2013, driven by emerging markets including smaller cities in China. Growth in content per box, however, was limited by technological improvements. I estimated content/box growth at 9% in 2012 and 3% in 2013 (due to Windows 8 efficiencies relative to Windows 7).

Server Unit Demand – Servers represented a growing market for DRAM both in units and content per box. With the shift towards cloud computing and centralized data storage, there was an ongoing secular growth story in server DRAM demand. Based on MSFT, HPQ, ORCL and others' demand projections for servers, I assumed about 7.5% unit growth in 2012 and 2013 and 15-16% content/box growth in both years.

Tablet/Ultrabook Demand – I estimated high growth for DRAM in tablets and ultrabooks because the iPad and

Kindle Fire were selling well and reviews on Ultrabooks had been good. Based on estimates for all three, I assumed 65% unit growth in 2012 and 61% in 2013. Content per box was still very low at an estimated .53GB/device in 2011. I assumed this almost doubled to 0.98 in 2012 and increased by another 50% to 1.45 in 2013.

Phone Demand – I assumed smart phone growth of 34% in 2012 and 30% in 2013 and feature phone growth of 7.3% in 2012 and 8.9% in 2013. For smart phones, there is substantial value to increased content per box, which I modelled at 22% in 2012 and 21% in 2013. In feature phones, there is not as much need to increase content/box, so I assume about 20% each year. Through all of this, I calculated supply and demand, below.

	2004	2005	2006	2007	2008	2009	2010	2011E	2012E	2013E
DRAM Revenue ($millions)	25,072	25,171	34,248	30,765	22,725	22,624	39,103			
YoY % (Revenue)		0.4%	36.1%	-10.2%	-26.1%	-0.4%	72.8%			
Unit Shipment (Millions 1Gb Equiv)	1,102	1,838	2,876	5,270	8,539	10,568	15,232	22,007	29,403	39,818
YoY%		66.8%	56.5%	83.3%	62.0%	23.8%	44.1%	44.5%	33.6%	35.4%
ASP (1Gb Equiv)	$22.75	$13.70	$11.91	$5.84	$2.66	$2.14	$2.57	$1.05	$0.85	$0.70
YoY % (1Gb Equiv prices)		-39.8%	-13.0%	-51.0%	-54.4%	-19.6%	19.9%	-59.1%	-19.0%	-17.6%
Blended DRAM Cost						$1.99	$1.64	$1.24	$0.96	$0.77
YoY % (1Gb Equiv prices)							-17.6%	-24.4%	-22.9%	-19.4%
Supply (mn Gb)			2,876	5,270	8,539	10,568	15,232	22,007	29,403	39,818
Demand (mn Gb)			2,965	5,108	8,314	10,707	15,248	21,065	27,734	36,218
YoY%				72%	63%	29%	42%	38%	32%	31%
Supply/Demand			-3%	3%	3%	-1%	0%	4%	6%	10%

Wafer Starts (12" Equiv)	2004	2005	2006	2007	2008	2009	2010	2011E
Samsung	2,469	2,261	3,408	4,155	4,763	4,288	4,528	4,528
		-8%	51%	22%	15%	-10%	6%	0%
Hynix	1,384	1,960	2,313	3,693	3,986	3,627	3,627	3,627
		42%	18%	60%	8%	-9%	0%	0%
Micron	1,205	1,418	1,207	1,463	1,327	2,084	2,138	2,138
		18%	-15%	21%	-9%	57%	3%	0%
Elpida	579	767	2,207	2,229	2,304	2,460	2,520	2,280
		33%	188%	1%	3%	7%	2%	-10%
Total Capacity				15,859	17,042	13,082	15,758	14,851
					7%	-23%	20%	-6%

The crux of the Elpida short case is displayed in the charts above. Historically, demand had grown, so the DRAM manufacturers simply cut wafer manufacturing production (remember, supply still grew as they moved to the newer node) so that supply and demand remained about the same. However, at the time of my analysis, I believed cutting wafer manufacturing would be insufficient for balancing supply/demand as demand began to plateau. Even with massively reduced wafer manufacturing levels, the migration to the new manufacturing node would still result in significant supply growth.

After conversations with industry experts and economic theory around the Five Forces framework, I believed that ASPs would decline to the cash cost per chip of fringe manufacturers. As per the chart above which lists blended costs and ASPs for the four major manufacturers, for Hynix, Micron and Elpida, Q3 2011 ASPs (pretty much the low) were at about the cash cost for each producer (assuming depreciation of $0.30-$0.40 per Gb based on different process node sizes). What this means is that in a cyclical downturn, fringe players will sell at the Nash Equilibrium point (cash cost), meaning a competitive race to the bottom until they hit their breakeven marginal cash cost. The overall cost includes depreciation, which is not a cash expense, so we can subtract my estimate of depreciation per Gb to arrive at my cash cost. Given Samsung's massive cost advantage, I believed that the lowest ASP the industry would reach was around the cash costs for the three other producers, excluding Samsung (Hynix, Micron and Elpida). Samsung would simply produce at full capacity and sell all its units into the market at any ASP. i.e. they did not need to lower price to their cash costs since they could sell all their units at the cash costs of their three major competitors and still make a decent operating margin because they were the lowest cost producer. Based on this, I estimated a blended cost in 2011 of $1.38 per Gb for Hynix, Micron and Elpida and an ASP of $1.05 (the difference being depreciation which is not a cash cost).

In order to understand how 2012 and 2013 ASPs would play out, I assumed Samsung would fully supply into the market regardless of price. Thus, I needed to look at industry supply/demand ex-Samsung since, over the longer term, companies operating with a cost structure well above ASPs should exit the industry. I determined that the supply of Hynix, Micron and Elpida was insufficient to meet full demand (ex-Samsung) in 2012 so the next lowest-cost producer, Nanya, would also sell into the market. In this analysis, I assume that Powerchip, Promos and the other small, higher-cost producers would exit the industry in 2012.

	2012	2013
Hynix	6,880	9,547
Micron	3,261	5,111
Elpida	5,359	6,605
Total	15,500	21,263
Demand	16,726	20,699
Supply/Demand	-7.3%	2.7%
Blended Cost	1.07	0.89
Nanya	1,995	2,245
Imbalance w Nanya	4.6%	13.6%

At this point, I needed to include some capacity from Nanya, also factoring their cash costs into my ASP assumptions. Given about $0.90 cash costs for Nanya (they were at about $1.28 in total costs and have a higher average node size, hence greater depreciation), I assumed that ASPs were at about $0.85 in 2012. In 2013, given node migrations discussed above, Hynix, Micron and Elpida could fulfill all ex-Samsung demand, hence a downward shift in ASPs towards their blended cost curves. Given that the industry would become more rational with less suppliers, I assumed that ASPs would fall to about blended cost minus maintenance capex. I would assume this to be the standard for long term ASPs.

Now that I had a sense of ASPs going forward based on each manufacturer's cost curves and the demand situation, I moved on to determining the Elpida-specific investment case.

Based on the ASP analysis, I estimated FY2011 at a $0.92 ASP. I further modelled Elpida ASPs 8% and 5% below the industry in FY2012 and FY2013, respectively, because I estimated that they sold more commodity DRAM than server DRAM (which was slightly higher ASP). I fully worked out cost of sales based on the supplier cost curve assumptions previously discussed. I further estimated opex and taxes based on the recent past. I estimated capex assuming the cost of new equipment for the next node but no capacity increases. The result showed continued losses in free cash flow, as shown below.

	2010	2011	2012	2013
Free Cash Flow	52,955	-78,756	-23,504	-28,217

SETUP AND CONCLUSION: HOW WOULD ELPIDA FUND LOSSES AND HOW DID I VALUE THE EQUITY?

SYNDICATED LOAN CONVERTED TO CONVERTIBLE DEBT

Most of Elpida's Syndicated Loan was coming due in April 2012. The loan was owed to the Development Bank of Japan (DBJ), the sovereign bank owned by the Japanese government. At the time, certain Japanese LCD (liquid crystal display screen) companies owed loans to the DBJ through money-losing subsidiaries. Each LCD company pooled its assets and converted the DBJ's stake into equity in the new company. In a best-case scenario for Elpida, I assumed the government would step in through the DBJ and convert the syndicated loan to convertible debt at a high strike price and low interest rate. Elpida's current business/capital structure prevented it from issuing additional secured or unsecured debt. If the government stepped in, it would own the best part of the capital structure with an equity kicker and a claim to its assets in case of bankruptcy. While the German government did not bail out Qimonda (another semiconductor manufacturer in a precarious financial situation), the mindset of the Japanese government had always been more protectionist. Given the small size of Elpida, the government could have easily bailed them out, in which case, current shareholders' equity would continue to decline but they would not go bankrupt.

In this scenario, I assumed the DBJ would issue a convert at a nominal interest rate of 0.25% for the 45blnY coming due in FY2011 and the 163.3blnY coming due in FY2012. The result was shareholders' equity available to common shareholders of 102blnY at the end of FY2011, 75blnY at the end of FY2012 and 10blnY at the end of FY2013. Consensus tended to use shareholders' equity as a proxy for valuation in these businesses. Thus, as a going concern or continued operating company, downside was significant. In a bankruptcy scenario, I had downside to 0, thus a great short in late 2011!

	2009	2010	2011	2012	2013
Ordinary Shareholders Equity	233,924	256,063	102,122	75,277	10,893
Ordinary Shareholders Equity/Share	861	942	376	277	40
Downside to Stock Price			-12.8%	-35.7%	-90.7%

In early January 2012, rumors swirled that amidst Elpida's precarious financial situation, the Japanese government attempted to negotiate an Elpida partnership with Toshiba, combined with some sort of government bailout. In late January 2012, the press reported that Elpida may sell its main plant to maintain solvency and possibly accept an investment from Micron. Finally, in February 2012, Elpida filed for bankruptcy as the Japanese government refused to bail them out while believing the jobs could be protected through the bankruptcy process.

TENETS MANIFESTED IN ELPIDA

During the idea sourcing phase, I learned about Elpida through industry research and putting myself out there. I highlighted the Elpida short partly because it is very different from many of the other shorts discussed in this book. Commodity manufacturing businesses (whether textile mills or DRAM manufacturing facilities) require an in-depth analysis of the industry's cost curve because the products are almost totally the same, so one manufacturer's actions affect the others. Mapping out the cost of production to determine unit economics and position on the industry cost curve is imperative in assessing supply/demand, as discussed above. What made Elpida a great short was the poor unit economics/placement on the cost curve combined with an inflection in demand and near-term maturities.

CHAPTER 8: AMBARELLA

SHORTING AN INNOVATOR WITH SLOWING GROWTH IN HIGH MARGIN PRODUCTS AND INCREASED COMPETITION

The case of the Ambarella short offers insight into a situation where the fundamental thesis played out exactly as I predicted, but the stock did not move down significantly. As expected, the company experienced a structural decline in earnings power while trying to diversify itself from a single-product innovator with a dilemma into a large and growing market. While the stock did not go down significantly, I'd do the same work and short AMBA again in retrospect, i.e. the process was correct even if the result was not favorable. The reader, however, can decide whether he or she might have avoided AMBA based on the information uncovered on their new product set after initially shorting. In addition, the reader can see the importance of a strong margin of safety based on a high multiple on an over-earning business. Lacking such a margin of safety, I would have lost money on the AMBA short rather than simply breaking even.

INTRODUCTION

Ambarella (AMBA) designs semiconductor chips for security surveillance cameras (40% of revenue in 2015/2016), action cameras (35% of revenue), automotive dashboard/bumper cameras (10% of revenue) and movie studio cameras (6% of revenue). AMBA's chips, very simply, turn moving video into lots of 1's and 0's on a recording device (compress the video) and reconvert the 1's and 0's back into a moving video when the device is plugged into a television or computer when watched (decompression).

AMBA's chip garnered significant market share and growth because its algorithm could turn the video into fewer 1's and 0's than competitors. By using less battery power and storage than comparable chips, it increased the battery life, storage capacity, and efficiency of cameras, particularly beneficial to action cameras. Many action cameras including GoPro, which I was also short at the time, exclusively used AMBA chips. As the action camera industry shifted to higher resolution levels (1080p to 4K), AMBA continued to steal share from inferior competitors.

IDEA SOURCING

I became familiar with AMBA at the Consumer Electronics Show (Empathy and IPO Monitoring Tenets) shortly after its IPO. I revisited the company a couple years later as a potential short after successfully shorting one of its customers, a security surveillance camera manufacturer that used AMBA's chips. I had shorted the manufacturer based on increased Chinese security camera competition. Competitive Chinese products utilized a Huawei chip which was lower quality but came at a significant discount to AMBA's chip, allowing the cameras to sell at a 50% price discount relative to those with AMBA chips. In addition, I noticed AMBA's management selling all of their founders' stock while also exercising and simultaneously selling options that expired far in the future (an extremely bearish sign – if they believed the stock would increase, they would sell those options later given the long-term expiry). AMBA definitely piqued my interest enough to move it to the diligence phase.

DILIGENCE

Through detailed conversations with experts, I identified two threats to AMBA. First, the shift from high to low-end IP security surveillance and action cameras. Companies like GPRO, which I was also short at the time, were facing increased competition, and together with surveillance cameras made up 75% of AMBA's revenue. Second, AMBA was facing increased competition from other chip manufacturers.

As recently as 12 years beforehand, the security surveillance market consisted of only analog CCTV cameras—that is, a single camera connected directly to a monitor and tape recorder. Several large manufacturers controlled the market through a network of integrators which had strong relationships with end customers. Over the following six-eight years, the market transitioned from analog to IP-based cameras integrated with a single hard disk drive recording device and a video management system (VMS).

Given the slow-moving nature of the entrenched analog companies and the limited technological sophistication of the integrators, the incumbents were slow to change, and a host of new IP camera manufacturers took share, many using AMBA's chips. However, these companies primarily served mid-to-high-end customers, the precise market segment where the transition from analog to digital was already largely complete. According to Axis (the largest European IP security camera manufacturer), the high-end of the market was 95% penetrated by IP-based solutions by 2014. Therefore, while the overall industry might still have grown at a 15% annual rate, most of that growth would occur at the very low-end. The low-end of the market is mainly made up of small customers like gas stations and convenience stores that are highly price sensitive and install only 1 to 10 720p cameras. My research indicated that AMBA's share of the market would decrease as the mid/high-end of the overall market should slow to the low single digits relative to 30%+ at the low-end, AMBA would face increasing pricing competition at the chip level.

Further supporting the AMBA short thesis, competition from Asian manufacturers was increasing as industry innovation hit a standstill for both chip and camera manufacturers. While AMBA had historically offered new products (720p, then 1080p, then 4K with increasing frame rates per second) six months ahead of competitors, 4K at 60 frames per second was the last innovation in the industry since the human eye could not tell the difference between 4K and 8K in anything smaller than a movie screen. According to multiple security camera manufacturers and integrators, customers were unwilling to replace 1080p solutions for 4K, and low-end customers, where demand was growing, opted for the less expensive 720p cameras which used $5 ASP chips (vs. $10 at AMBA). The CEO of Avigilon, a camera producer, sums it up: "What we think is happening now is that a commoditization of hardware, particularly IP and megapixel cameras, is underway. There is an increasing influx of typically Asian-made, low-cost cameras hitting the market, which is to be expected and is not something we're surprised by".

The lower-end cameras favored the less expensive $5 ASP chips. To remain competitive, leading camera manufacturers like Samsung, Hikvision, and Dahua had to cut costs and the high-end market increasingly consolidated. Panasonic had recently acquired Video Insight and Canon had recently acquired Axis. Jon Cropley, principal analyst for video surveillance and security services for IHS, echoed the effects of these recent trends: "The year 2014 has been one of the most interesting—and disruptive—in recent memory, for both the professional and consumer video surveillance industries...A sharp decline in the cost of semiconductor components has ushered in a new era of price competition, and the competitive landscape has shifted, with merger-and-acquisition activity affecting some of the leading global product and software vendors."

Driven by the shift towards lower-end cameras and the price pressure from leading and high-end camera manufacturers, incremental growth (i.e. most of AMBA/competitor sales) should primarily come at the low-end with $5 ASPs and 30% gross margins (calculated using AMBA estimated chip cost of \$3.50 and \$5 competitor ASPs). Lower chip pricing by multiple new entrants had spurred a competitive race to the bottom.

Confident that the industry expert opinion suggested challenges to AMBA, I moved forward to estimating earnings and valuation. I assessed the direction of the security surveillance market, action camera market, and chip market to estimate earnings power.

My analysis of the highly-fragmented security surveillance camera market contains imperfect data given fragmentation, but I found that there were many highly price sensitive/elastic customers like convenience stores, gas stations, and extremely low traffic areas that would convert only from analog to digital at a comparable price.

The elastic customers in commercial, retail, banking and manufacturing did not convert from analog to digital as the market grew from 2009-2014 and as IP (digital) grew from 15% of the overall market to an expected 51% in 2016. The bottom line is that the 50% of the market that would upgrade in the future would do so at a significantly lower camera and chip price. Thus, I concluded as technological innovation slows and sales shift to Chinese camera vendors favoring local chip vendors, security camera sales at the high-end would slow and AMBA's sales and margins should decline substantially.

Second, I considered the action camera market. Demand for action cameras, like for security surveillance cameras, was slowing at the high-end with increased low-end competition. The success of GPRO's IPO and lofty consensus expectations partially drove Wall St's misvaluation of AMBA. Bulls estimated GPRO would maintain its 75% market share and increase units from 4M in 2014/2014 10M by 2018 but failed to account for increasing competition. Novatek-enabled action cameras ranging from $70 (1080p30/720p60) to $175 (1080p60) were low-end competitors, especially internationally, while Sony's AS1000V (4K30) with OIS and GPS were taking share at the high-end.

If I assumed consensus estimates for action camera unit growth of 25-30% would hold over the medium term, chip prices should decline as low-end cameras containing cheaper chips by AMBA and its competitors capture a disproportionate percentage of GPRO's unit growth. Additional upside to the short might also come from GPRO dual sourcing AMBA with a competitor. The shift to low-end action cameras, as with surveillance cameras, would further impair AMBA's earnings power.

Lastly, as alluded to above, competition for AMBA's chips, themselves, was increasing. As previously mentioned, AMBA became the sole-sourced chip supplier for GoPro (and the security camera market) because it was first to market with encode/decode software and an HD solution at the leading manufacturing node. AMBA remained the market leader and unveiled the industry's only 4K60 chip at 14nm

in October 2014 (to be manufactured at the end of 2015
and integrated into products by 2H 2016). Though they beat
competitors by at least nine months (except Sony), their lead
was less valuable at the growing low-end of the bifurcating
security and action camera markets. Similarly, though they
maintained the power advantage from manufacturing at the
leading edge, the only market it provided any use in was for
$499+ action cameras. With a 12+ hour battery life at 28nm
at 1080p60, the only market where 14nm provided any
useful power benefits was at 4K, or the market for $499+
action cameras. This market would likely represent only
about 20-30% of AMBA's action camera segment (8-10%
of AMBA's overall revenue) as the low-end (720p/1080p)
represented most of the incremental growth going forward.
At the time of diligence with experts, I uncovered competitive chips at Hisilicon, Novatek, Geo Semiconductor, Texas
Instruments, Lofty, Chipworks and Allwinner, along with
internally produced chips at Sony (security/action cameras),
Dahua, Hikvision and Axis.

FRAMING THE BULL CASE

In early 2015, a bulge bracket investment bank raised
its price target on AMBA from $50 to $65 based on 24x
CY2016 EPS of $2.70 reflecting higher investor enthusiasm
for GoPro/Xiaomi wearable cameras, high growth prospects for cop cams and growing traction in quadcopters/
drones and automotive cameras. They justified a high multiple by estimating that the company would grow long-term

at 27-30%/year. My estimated EPS accretion based on these new markets, however, failed to suggest that level of growth.

VALUATION AND MODELING

Revenue Source	Indicator	FY16 Assumption	FY17-18 Assumption
Action Cameras	Volume (units)	Consensus for GPRO	15% growth for GPRO
	ASP ($)	Decline, based on the mix of $8 ASP chips and $12 ASP chips shifting from 90/10 to 50/50	15% annual degradation
Security Cameras	Volume (units)	25% YOY growth at start of year decreasing to 15% by end of year	15% growth along
	ASP ($)	$9	10-15% decline to $5.80 from FY16 to end of FY18
Infrastructure	Revenue ($)	Flat	Flat
Automobile Cameras	Revenue ($)	13% annual revenue growth	13% annual revenue growth
Other Cameras	Revenue ($)	45% annual revenue growth due to potential new end markets (drones, cop cameras)	45% annual revenue growth
Cost	Indicator	FY16 Assumption	FY17-18 Assumption
Chips	Cost/Chip ($)	4% annual decline due to decreasing manufacturing costs, from $3.75 in FY14/15 to $3.25 by FY18	4% annual decline
R&D	Spending	15-18% growth in FY16 due to migration to next manufacturing node, as discussed by management	

This resulted in, by FY2017, $1.59 in EPS and $1.05 in FY18 vs. consensus at $2.80 for FY17 and $3 for FY18, hence I estimated the stock should easily fall to $18 (18x $1.05).

SETUP AND CONCLUSION

I shorted the stock in the low $50s and the AMBA roller coaster ride began.

In March 2015, AMBA reported FQ1 guidance of $64-68m vs. consensus of $59m. Xiaomi had launched an action camera utilizing a high-end AMBA chip. The introduction of new product that used high-end AMBA chips was contrary to my short thesis and the stock rallied to the mid $60s. However, continued diligence on my end showed that Hisilicon had introduced a high-end chip that it was pricing 30-50% below AMBA, so I stuck with the short, especially given the valuation.

By May 2015, AMBA stock had rallied into the $80s as the
sell-side continued to increase their price targets in positive research reports citing growth in another unexpected
market for AMBA, quadcopters/drones, along with a potential acquisition of AMBA by QCOM. I believed a QCOM
acquisition was unlikely because QCOM already designed
technology exactly like AMBA's into smartphone applications processor chips (the brains of our smartphones). Should
QCOM choose to get into the same markets as AMBA, they
could easily design a 'dumber' chip than a smartphone
apps processor but with their own encode/decode technology to sell into the camera market. It was doubtful to
me that they would pay a very high multiple and billions
of dollars to acquire AMBA vs. spending tens of millions
to recreate the technology and run it through their much
better distribution network.

By June 2015, AMBA guided to FQ2 revenue of $79-83m
vs. consensus of $68.4m and gross margins of 63.5-65% vs.
consensus of 61.9% based on growth across the board with
strength in drones. The stock rallied into the high $90s!
At this point, the sell-side began raising their price targets
into the $110s, citing likely growth from unknown new end
markets and an extrapolation of current strength in revenue
and margins. It's always important to constantly re-assess
our theses when we are involved, especially in a case like
this where the stock had doubled on me and my thesis of a
slowdown in earnings based on a move to the low-end was
clearly not playing out. At this point, I undertook a TAM
(total addressable market) analysis to estimate earnings

power from some of these new markets that I had missed in my initial analysis. My thought was to sanity-check whether they could justify a move up of about +$50/AMBA share.

Drones	
Market Size	2,153
14-18 CAGR	32%
AMBA Share	50%
AMBA Units	1,077
AMBA ASP	$15
Revenue	16,148
Incremental Net Income Margin	50%
Incremental EPS	0.24

Assuming a 32% CAGR in drones through 2018 and 25% share to AMBA (since the largest drone company, Parrot, used an internal chip), even at the high-end of ASPs, drones would generate only $0.07 in incremental EPS to AMBA.

Copcams	
Market Size	1,750
Camera Attach	75%
Camera Units	1,313
AMBA Share	50%
AMBA Units	656
AMBA ASP	$10
Revenue	6,563
Incremental Net Income Margin	40%
Incremental EPS	0.08

Similarly, given the recent alleged police brutality issues and recent share wins by AMBA in copcams, the market began pricing in continued growth in this segment. Similarly, I assumed a very aggressive 75% attach rate in cameras to every cop (1.75m) in the US/Western Europe or just over 1.3m units (annually!) and a 50% share for AMBA since Taser was also in the market and had great relationships with police departments in the US. I estimated similar ASPs and margins to drones. The result was only an additional $0.08 in EPS.

As such, it was hard for me to understand how $0.15, or even $0.30-0.50 in case I was missing another 3-4 new markets, could justify a $40 increase in AMBA's stock. I stuck with my gut and stayed short AMBA.

By September 2015, when AMBA guided FQ3 revenue of $90-93m vs. consensus of $92.3m, I saw the extent of lofty estimates priced in when the stock declined 6.8% (it was still in the high $80s) as the company could not maintain its 'beat and raise', i.e. beat revenue for the quarter and raise guidance vs. consensus to support the high stock price. Momentum finally broke and the stock dropped to the $60s through the end of 2015. Lesson learned – continue to reassess the thesis, especially if Mr. Market does not agree and maintain conviction if you believe you are right even as the stock goes against you. That said, while the stock came back down close to the price at which I had initially shorted, I hadn't made money yet so I debated whether I should break even, cover and move on or continue to stay short.

Despite the unexpected new end markets, the thesis was in-
tact around the initial end markets in security surveillance
and action cameras, even if delayed, while the new end
markets would not add too much in incremental revenue/
earnings power. Accordingly, I stuck with the short thesis.
I maintained conviction especially after AMBA guided
FQ4 on 12/3/2015 revenue of $65-67.5m vs. consensus of
$76.3m. The street gave the company a pass because the
weakness came from GPRO which was well known at the
time, but I believed the company would only get weaker and
future earnings would be impaired, as per my thesis.

In mid-January 2016, GPRO significantly missed revenue
and volume estimates based on declining high-end demand
as I had predicted and AMBA dropped into the mid $40s.
On the heels of GPRO, when AMBA reported earnings in
early March 2016, they guided FQ1 to $55-57m in reve-
nue vs. consensus of $62.4m based on declines in the action
camera market. AMBA also guided to $60-66m in FQ2 vs.
consensus of $67.5m in June 2016 based on a decline in Sony
revenue due to the Japanese earthquake.

Over the course of the rest of 2016 and 2017, AMBA continued to slightly beat/hit/miss street consensus and the stock
bounced around in the $50s until September 2017. Then,
the company guided FY18 revenue growth to be between
negative 7% and negative 3%, down from previous guidance of growth between plus or minus 3%. My thesis finally
began to play out with consensus FY18 EPS dropping from
$3/share when I first shorted the stock to $2/share.

All said and done, AMBA reported FY19 EPS of $0.73, just about exactly the number I estimated back in 2014/2015 when I first shorted the stock. That said, the company began to discuss a new segment that captured street attention, chips for autonomous cars utilizing computer/machine vision/artificial intelligence. The new announcement caused the street to keep price targets high on a multiple basis (i.e. 50-60x $1 in EPS for a company with declining revenue) based on the opportunity to sell into autonomous vehicles in 2022+. Despite nailing the fundamental thesis, the company continued to sell a very different story to the sell-side based on the buzzwords of today: autonomous driving, machine learning and artificial intelligence.

At the time of writing this book, I remain short AMBA. Management has been disciplined with going after only high-end camera chip business, limiting gross margin compression despite declines in revenue. The revenue declines, however, have been so large that they still hit my very low FY18/19 EPS which I had estimated at the time of the initial short, significantly lower than consensus. GPRO also dual sourced in 2017 with Socionext. I had not uncovered Socionext in any competitor diligence before they won GPRO, which is telling that there are many other competitors in the core camera chip business. Meanwhile, management continues to 'sell' to investors their machine vision (aka computer vision (CV)) autonomous car story while also selling their stock in the company. I believe competition is fierce in the autonomous car chip business and AMBA's first mover/technological advantage no longer exists.

AMBA has been a thrilling ride and a great lesson in the risks in short selling in a low-interest rate fueled bubble. As long as people continue to believe, the perception can stay alive for a long time. We must have patience as the thesis changes and any drop in the stock takes longer. However, another great lesson from the AMBA short is to continually reevaluate positions. Every day, I wake up and look at the Papyrus Capital portfolio and determine whether my longs and shorts make sense at the current time. In the case of AMBA, it made sense when I initiated the short in the $50s. When it rallied to $100 and I reassessed the short scenario, it still made sense given the limited additional earnings power from copcams and drones. As it dropped and my/the initial fundamental thesis began to play out, the short continued to look good. Only time will tell if I am right or wrong but the AMBA case shows the importance of nailing the fundamental thesis in order to provide a margin of safety on shorts. If I hadn't had such a wide margin of safety here, I could have lost money rather than breaking even as a perfect storm of sentiment so significantly expanded the multiple.

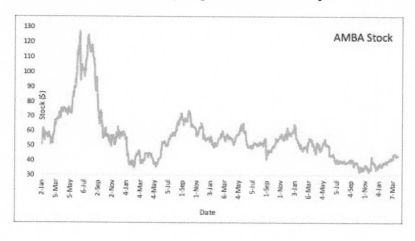

CHAPTER 9: PASSES WHERE TENETS BROKE DOWN

Just like reporting a-posteriori on businesses that fail, it's easy to match shorts that worked with a list of tenets in hindsight. As such, in this last chapter, I walk through (in much shorter detail) names that passed the initial idea sourcing phase but failed to pass the diligence phase. In these cases, I recognized the sunk cost of my initial work and moved on. When investing, it's very easy to develop a commitment and consistency bias and go long or short just because we have done a ton of work, whether or not it's actually a good long/short. Generating a great return demands the discipline and patience to short only when an idea passes diligence. Time may show that I was wrong to pass on some of these potential shorts, but an investor should follow a process and be confident in his or her thesis rather than forcing an outcome.

As previously discussed, the tenets should be used as a checklist for shorts. While it's not necessary for all the tenets to hold true in a good short, it's unwise to short if just one tenet holds true or if some tenets are directly contradicted.

MOTOROLA SOLUTIONS INC (MSI)

MSI sells walkie-talkies and operates exclusive narrow-band walkie-talkie networks primarily for US-based first responders. MSI contracts with municipalities to provide first responders with these walkie-talkies and sets up radio networks for the handsets to connect around the town/city. In 2017, the federal government initiated a new nationwide public safety network, called FirstNet, with the intention of moving all public safety communication onto this network. FirstNet would render MSI's individual networks obsolete and threaten the company's razor/razor-blade business model. MSI sells their walkie-talkies for thousands of dollars ($5-10k) and very high gross margins due to its monopoly/duopoly position in operating the network. FirstNet, on the other hand, would cost $800-1,000 for a smartphone to connect, threatening MSI's earnings and 24x PE. I monitored the situation since the early stages of FirstNet in 2017 when AT&T was awarded a contract to host the network. I began assessing the short case in late 2018 when I noticed significant insider sales by many members of management, including almost $75m in sales by the CEO in 2018, alone. Given the likely disruption of MSI's high-margin handset revenue by FirstNet phones at a lower price point/many competitive products, I started the diligence phase. However, I identified two features of MSI's network that could prove to differentiate it enough from FirstNet to maintain its position. First, MSI's walkie-talkies have a push-to-talk feature, a one-button-touch to connect first responders. FirstNet would not incorporate the feature until late 2019. Upon speaking to several purchasing managers of first responders' equipment in different municipalities around the country, I also learned that MSI differentiates itself by the ability to handle mission critical voice, offering coverage everywhere. Mission critical voice is crucial in emergency situations like a cop calling in for backup or a firefighter needing to communicate in a burning building. FirstNet, importantly, does not have plans to offer this critical service due to a lack of technological capability. According to a few conversations, this is the case because MSI's devices are 16x the power levels of FirstNet phones and support only narrow-band voice, whereas smartphones on FirstNet support data and apps. When 16x the power is used just for voice, the device provides more coverage than a smartphone. A SWAT team three levels below ground on a mission is more likely to get voice coverage through MSI's network than through FirstNet's. Municipalities are unlikely to give up this key feature and take a risk on emergency communication, so I tabled MSI despite a high multiple on extremely high gross margins and significant insider selling. While FirstNet may still disrupt MSI, I don't think it will happen until FirstNet resolves the coverage issue. The short failed on two important tenets: impending competition and low customer switching costs.

UBIQUITY NETWORKS INC (UBNT)

UBNT, a short on which I ultimately passed, is an interesting contrast in technology hardware compared to INVN or FIO, discussed earlier. UBNT sells networking equipment into the WISP (wireless internet service provider) market for the purpose of providing rural areas with internet service. Locations without broadband internet from cable or DSL can use UBNT receivers. The UBNT receivers connect to a broadband gateway and emit a signal over unlicensed spectrum to homes or businesses in the surrounding area, providing internet service. UBNT also sells the router equipment that can be set up on lampposts around the town to connect to the gateway and provide the town with wireless internet service. A thoughtful entrepreneur with equipment from UBNT, a satellite dish, and leased wholesale broadband from a satellite provider can connect a town to wireless internet service. UBNT also sells mesh wireless routers (routers with multiple end points to create a mesh network for seamless handoff for office buildings, university campuses, etc) and security surveillance cameras. I identified UBNT as a potential short for multiple reasons. UBNT sells a commoditized hardware product and has a small end market, as there aren't too many areas of the world rural enough for their internet service product. The company has only 200 employees and no salesforce or significant R&D spend, and its routers/security cameras break after a few years according to customer reviews. The company is managed by a loud CEO who tried to buy a basketball team and had a high valuation at 5-6x revenue. While, on the surface, UBNT has many of the characteristics of my other successful tech hardware shorts, the diligence phase showed that UBNT had a strong enough distribution network to prevent me from shorting the company. While UBNT has no internal salesforce, they have a close relationship with a large network of global distributors. Their distributors sell their products primarily to small businesses in developed and emerging markets. While the WISP product might be saturated within that distributor network, their model allows them to create new products, price them much lower than competitor products (because they do not need to pay an internal salesforce) and sell them through their outsourced relationships. This was UBNT's strategy for its wireless mesh routers and security surveillance cameras. UBNT developed and sold surveillance cameras at 40% gross margins vs. competitors at 50-60% and was able to capture the low-end of the market. Accordingly, even if customer, competitor, and supplier analyses suggested high competition for UBNT, the company could easily invent a new product and quickly sell it through its distributors, as per Porter's Five Forces, where customer concentration is extremely low. The short failed on three fronts: it's a low cost producer, some customers love the products (due to price) and the bear case is very well-known on Wall Street.

2U INC (TWOU)

TWOU is an online education support services provider. The company partners with leading universities like Georgetown, UNC, and USC to manage their online graduate degree programs. TWOU handles the technology backend and funds student recruitment, startup, and operating costs. In exchange for running the online programs, TWOU receives a revenue share in the range of 60% of online tuition. Contracts are created with a set number of years with the potential to renew at expiry. I became familiar with TWOU when they had an IPO in 2014 and revisited the business in 2018 when insiders rampantly sold stock. My diligence phase revealed that TWOU faced competition from companies like Noodle, which accepted revenue shares as low as 30-40%. When contracts came up for renewal, universities might switch to competitors, having already benefited from TWOU's marketing dollars to create value around the online degree programs. I assessed the unit economics of TWOU's programs using primary and secondary source documents and concluded that the very positive unit economics (long program durations and high revenue share) were likely to change in the face of competition. With declining unit economics and limited visibility on contract renewals, my DCF showed 50-70% downside on a very expensive stock. However, while a DCF analysis makes sense in theory, the metrics Wall Street pays attention to had not started to turn. Wall Street looked solely at revenue growth, and my conversations led me to believe revenue would continue to grow despite TWOU's potential challenges. Specifically, they could strike contracts with a shorter duration and high upfront revenue share (to boost near-term revenue) with a potential future decline in the revenue share rate. This would mean beating revenue estimates in the near-term even if the unit economics broke down over the longer-term. Given the growing online degree market, the declining unit economics would not factor into earnings for many years. The tenet of switching costs was also instrumental in my decision – because TWOU hosts backend content, billing, and lead generation, the switching cost for a university may be higher than it would seem once a contract expired. While TWOU was a great short on the surface, I eventually passed on it because the Wall Street metrics didn't turn and the switching cost for customers could have been higher than expected.

TWILIO INC (TWLO)

TWLO is a communications software company that hosts switching facilities in the cloud to allow their customers to mass text message or host voice (over the internet) calling solutions for call centers. When we communicate with a Lyft driver, we call a TWLO number that routes through a datacenter to the phone of the driver. I started following TWLO after its IPO given significant insider selling, and it piqued my interest in late 2018 when Amazon integrated a calling feature into its cloud computing service. On top of this, Uber cut its TWLO service in late 2016 from 15% of TWLO revenue ($60m) to 5% of revenue ($20m) as they transitioned service to a competitor. Increased competition, limited earnings generation potential, low switching costs and a high valuation made TWLO seem like a great short. However, upon peeling back the onion further when speaking to industry experts, I learned that TWLO's novel approach to virtual switching offered a more robust system to any company that provided customer service. TWLO's switching software was integrated into Amazon Web Services (AWS) and phone lines in 100 countries. TWLO also provides customers with an API (application program interface) that can integrate voice calling and text messaging into apps for end-users. A large investment bank, for example, had integrated TWLO into its app to communicate with customers and can even incorporate compliance monitoring in the app through TWLO's software. Customer call centers also utilize TWLO to improve tracking and store more customer information than call centers using typical hard switch phone systems. TWLO customers love the product and gain a lot of value from it, leading me to believe Uber's shift from TWLO was a fluke, likely due to Uber's unique tech savviness. I refrained from shorting TWLO given the high switching costs and product customers love.

HUGO BOSS (BOSS)

BOSS is a provider of men's clothing (85% of revenue) and women's clothing (15% of revenue), trading at 22x LTM PE in late 2017 when I evaluated the short. I was drawn to BOSS by the high multiple, continued promotions in department stores/company owned stores, and a shift from formalwear to new, 'hip' technology-focused suit brands with minimal retail presence and lower cost production in Asia, like SuitSupply. Given that 50-60% of their revenue came from suits, the consumer shift piqued my interest. BOSS was not a high-end brand like LVMH that could command a high multiple due to franchise value, and it did not operate at the lower end with high volumes and distribution. In my mind, it operated in no man's land where competition was fierce, and the company had a weaker brand than low-end Armani or Zegna at the same price points. Based on the weak retail environment, I further assessed the promotional environment where continued 66% gross margins seemed high for a floundering retailer. The China growth story, however, deterred me from the short. Conversations and news articles lead me to see that the name 'Boss' connoted rising through the ranks. The connotation was important in a country so focused on luck, especially among an aspirational middle class. The number of followers of Hugo Boss on WeChat and Weibo dwarfed other brands targeting the middle class with a high-end, prestige brand. My work on Canada Goose and Moncler yielded similar conclusions around the strength of the brands with Chinese consumers. Bottom line – stay away from shorts with products consumers love, especially in China where the sheer number of new millionaires on social media can build a brand almost instantaneously.

VIASAT INC (VSAT)

Over the years, many public short-sellers have published theses on VSAT, a satellite-based broadband provider to homes in the rural US. One such short-seller published a report in mid-2017 stating that VSAT's addressable market of rural homes with no access to faster broadband speeds (cable, DSL, fiber) was exaggerated and over time, their business would decline as competitors with faster speeds stole share. This short-seller also claimed that VSAT generated no actual free cash flow. Naturally, I have no 'idea ego', so it doesn't matter if an idea comes from a screen, a friend, a public report or a college student. If the idea sounds interesting, I will investigate. Given my knowledge of the telecom space,

I was excited to dig into VSAT. Upon doing so, I found several flaws to the short thesis. First, the threat from cable, DSL, and fiber was not as strong as the thesis claimed. The cost to build out infrastructure to underserved households in the US is very expensive for any of these options. The FCC estimated the cost to deliver broadband to the 10-20m households in extremely remote areas (the far reaches of the Catskills or the Adirondacks, for example) at approximately $8-10k per home. With a cable company receiving $100/month in broadband revenue ($1,200/year) on an average life of four years for a customer and a 50% margin, spending $8-10k to receive $2,400 in cash flows over the life of the subscriber is even worse than the wooden vulture example! Even with a $500 government subsidy per home, the math does not work. On the other hand, if VSAT spends $450m to build a satellite that can service 1m subscribers, their cost to build out to a home is about $450 (plus some cost of the modem at the customer's home), constituting favorable economics. While VSAT does not generate free cash flow, as the short thesis mentioned, they are spending their cash on building new satellites which generates a good IRR. Given their large addressable market and limited competition, I believe the unit economics on a customer and IRRs on their capital spending on new satellites makes sense. They are investing today for the future. Despite the high valuation, I didn't short VSAT. Valuation alone does not make a great short, and the unit economics/competitive angle tenets for VSAT do not hold.

EPILOGUE

I hope you have enjoyed reading this book as much as I have enjoyed writing it. I also hope that following my tenets helps you avoid poor long investments and identify great shorts. I further hope that the combination of the process/tenets with the cases of shorts that do and do not work show you that no two shorts are the same and the work required to distill them down into the framework of the tenets and the Five Forces requires some creativity. That said, I hope that providing so many examples will give you a sense of the creative exercises involved in uncovering the patterns that determine a good short.

I look forward to seeing you in the trenches of short-selling!

ABOUT THE AUTHOR

Nitin Sacheti is the Founder and Portfolio Manager of Papyrus Capital, a long/short equity fund where he utilizes his short-selling tenets to protect downside for his investors.

Prior to founding Papyrus, Mr. Sacheti was a Senior Analyst/Principal with Equity Contribution at Charter Bridge Capital where he managed the firm's investments in the technology, media and telecom sectors as well as select consumer investments. Previously, Mr. Sacheti was a Senior Analyst at Cobalt Capital, managing the firm's technology, media and telecom investments and Tiger Europe Management.

Mr. Sacheti began his investment career in 2006 at Ampere Capital Management, a consumer, media, telecom and technology focused investment firm, initially as a Junior Analyst, later becoming Assistant Portfolio Manager. He graduated from the University of Chicago with a BA in Economics and was a visiting undergraduate student in Economics at Harvard University.